Revising Prose
Fourth Edition

Richard A. Lanham
University of California, Los Angeles

Allyn and Bacon
Boston · London · Toronto · Sydney · Tokyo · Singapore

Library of Congress Cataloging-in-Publication Data

Lanham, Richard A.
    Revising prose / Richard A. Lanham. -- 4th ed.
        p.   cm.
    Includes index.
    ISBN 0-205-30945-3 (pbk.)
    1. English language--Rhetoric.   2. English language--Style.
3. Editing.   I. Title.
PE1421.L297   1999
808'.042--dc21   99-27670
                                                              CIP

Printed in the United States of America

10 9 8 7 6 5 4 3 2 1   03 02 01 00 99

CONTENTS

PREFACE

Revising Prose differs from other writing texts. Let me emphasize these differences up front.

    1. About *revising*. True to its title, it is about *revising*; it does not deal with original composition. People often argue that writing cannot be taught, and if they mean that inspiration cannot be commanded nor laziness banished, then of course they are right. But stylistic analysis—revision—is something else, a method, not a mystical rite. How we compose— pray for the muse, marshal our thoughts, find willpower to glue backside to chair—these may be idiosyncratic, but revision belongs to the public domain. Anyone can learn it.

    In colleges and universities, revising is more common nowadays than it was when this book first appeared. Computers have made it much easier to do. Still, except in composition classes, instructors seldom require it or help students revise on their own. Nothing would improve student writing more than steady, detailed revision, but such revision is difficult to do, especially without guidance. The process deserves a book to itself. That's what *Revising Prose* tries to be.

    In the workplace to which school leads, revision usually poses more problems than original composition. At work the "student's dilemma," what to write about, hardly exists. The facts are there, the needs press hard, the arguments lie ready to hand, the deadline impends. The first draft assembles itself from the external pressures. You bat it out on a crowded plane flying back home from a meeting. Or you start with the draft a colleague has batted out. Then the sweat really begins: *revision*, commonly done in group settings. For much organizational writing, collective revision up through a hierarchy determines the final text. "All writing is rewriting," goes the cliché. OK. Here's the book for it. It offers a collective writing philosophy which a group can easily and quickly learn to share.

2. Translates "the Official Style" into English. A specific analytical and social premise informs *Revising Prose*: much bad writing today comes not from the conventional sources of verbal dereliction—sloth, ignorance, or native absence of mind—but from stylistic imitation. It is learned, an act of stylistic piety which imitates a single style, the bureaucratic style I have called the Official Style. This bureaucratic style dominates written discourse in our time, and beginning or harried or fearful writers adopt it as a protective coloration. So common a writing pattern deserves a separate focus, a book of its own. *Revising Prose* is about revising the Official Style into plain English.

There are signs that "the Official Style" may be going out of style. The Securities and Exchange Commission has started requiring that Initial Public Offerings in new companies be written in a plain style. President Clinton has even issued an executive order, in June 1998, requiring that federal agencies communicate in writing that is "clearer and easier to understand." Maybe this miracle will come to pass, but don't expect every "personal flotational device" to turn back into a "life jacket" overnight. If you are a bureaucrat who wants to take the new Executive Order to heart, though, *Revising Prose* is just the book for you.

3. Rule-based and self-teaching. *Revising Prose* was written to be a supplementary text for any course or task that required writing. The pressures of school or workplace rarely permit time off to take a special writing course. You need something useful right then. Again, a special book for this purpose seems justified. Because it addresses a single discrete

style, *Revising Prose* can be *rule-based* to a degree which prose
analysis rarely permits. This set of rules—the *Paramedic
Method* (PM)—in turn allows the book to be self-teaching.
   4. Useful in all jobs. Because the Official Style dominates
university, workplace, and government alike, *Revising Prose* can
work in all these contexts. Readers of earlier editions have
sometimes asked me whether *Revising Prose* addresses students
or teachers. It addresses the revising self in all of us—students,
teachers, and all other workers in the word. That revising self
is neither the writing self nor the reading self, but a third
one which uneasily combines both. Scholars who study children's language have argued that language-understanding and
language-using evolve as separate systems which only later
combine into full language competence. Revising tries to hold
these two different powers, two different selves, in mind at
once. That's what makes it so hard. In my experience, the land
of revision is an egalitarian place where pedagogical authority gives way to common perplexity. Thus *Revising Prose* addresses an audience including students and teachers but not
restricted to them. Used as directed, the *Paramedic Method*
works for anybody.
   5. Addresses the *electronic* word. If writing on an electronic screen has revolutionized prose composition and prose
style, nowhere has the revolution hit harder than in revision.
Revision is much easier to do on screen, more of it is being
done, and done in many new ways. Electronic text brings with
it a new stylistic theory as well as new means of moving
words around on an expressive surface. The fourth edition of
Revising Prose provides a beginner's guide to both theory and
practice.
   6. Saves time and money when used as directed. The bottom line for the workplace: the Paramedic Method, when used
as directed, saves time and money. Lots of it. Word-processing
time; fax time; duplicating time; file space; above all, reading
time. The Lard Factor of the Official Style usually runs about
50%, and eliminating it generates equivalent savings in all
these areas. The bottom line for students: you can say twice

as much in the space allotted you, and therefore get a better grade. When an instructor is ploughing through a batch of papers at two in the morning, a well-written, powerful train of thought shines out like the Holy Grail. And student time is money, too. So, times ten, is time in the workplace. The bottom line there is a big savings in the whole communications chain.

But the book has an even larger efficiency in view—stylistic self-consciousness. This verbal self-awareness, however generated, is like riding a bicycle: once learned, never forgotten. And stylistic self-consciousness changes how we read and write not only in a single bureaucratic register but across the board. From a particular focus, this book aims to teach a general skill with words, and to suggest that such a skill has moral implications, implications dealt with in the last chapter, "Why Bother?"

7. **Sentence-based.** The last point and the most important. *Revising Prose* focuses on the single sentence. Get the basic architecture of the English sentence straight, I think, and everything else will follow. Transposed up an octave toward generality, this book might have been called *The English Sentence*. We're analyzing in this book the microeconomics of prose. All our work together will be close-focus writing and what acousticians call "near-field" listening. Such close-focus work is as seldom performed as it is universally needed. We spend a great deal of time worrying about our verbal "P's and Q's" that we ought to spend worrying about our sentence architecture. That's where the big misunderstandings occur.

I've called my basic procedure for revision the Paramedic Method because it provides emergency therapy, a first-aid kit, a quick, self-teaching method of revision for people who want to translate the Official Style, their own or someone else's, into plain English. But it is only that—a first-aid kit. It's not the art of medicine. As with paramedicine in underdeveloped countries, it does not attempt to teach a full body of knowledge but only to diagnose and cure the epidemic disease. It won't answer, though at the end it addresses, the big question:

having the cure, how do you know when, or if, you should take it? For this you need the full art of prose medicine, a mature and reflective training in verbal self-awareness. I've addressed this larger stylistic domain in another book, *Analyzing Prose*.

To get the most out of *Revising Prose*, follow the PM. It works only if you *follow* it rather than *argue* with it. When it tells you to get rid of the prepositional phrases, get rid of them. Don't go into a "but, well, in this case, given my style, really I need to..." bob and weave. You'll never learn anything that way. The PM constitutes the center of this book. Use it. It is printed on a separate page in the front. Clip it out and tack it above your desk for easy reference.

Revising Prose has now been out in the world for two decades. Readers will want to know what is new in the fourth edition. Chapters 1–3 have been rewritten. Chapter 4 is new. I've revised the last two chapters as the changing times have required. Separately available are:

- a set of new interactive exercises, with discussion of each exercise and suggested revisions, and
- the *Revising Prose* video, a 30-minute video using animated print, sound, and color to depict revision in action.

Both may be ordered from Rhetorica, Inc., 927 Bluegrass Lane, Los Angeles, California 90049 (tel. 310-472-1577; fax 310-472-4757; email: rhetorica@aol.com).

A word about the last two items. Prose revision is an interactive process *par excellence,* best demonstrated and practiced dynamically. But the print medium—this book—can only describe it one step at a time. The interactive exercises allow you to try out, view on screen, various possibilities as you revise. The video shows revision as it happens.

In case you've forgotten what "active" and "passive," or even "noun" and "verb," mean, I've provided an appendix which defines the grammatical and rhetorical terms used in the text.

In this book, as in all my work, the editorial and scholarly eye of my wife, Carol Dana Lanham, has spared both reader and author many inconsistencies, gaffes, and stupidities. *Gratias ago.*

R. A. L.

REVISING
PROSE

THE
PARAMEDIC
METHOD

1. Circle the prepositions.
2. Circle the "is" forms.
3. Ask, "Where's the action?" "Who's kicking who?"
4. Put this "kicking" action in a simple (not compound) active verb.
5. Start fast—no slow windups.
6. Write out each sentence on a blank screen or sheet of paper and mark off its basic rhythmic units with a "/".
7. Mark off sentence lengths in the passage with a big "/" between sentences.
8. Read the passage aloud with emphasis and feeling.

CHAPTER 1

ACTION

Since we all live in a bureaucracy these days, it's not surprising that we end up writing like bureaucrats. Nobody feels comfortable writing simply "Bill loves Marge." The system requires something like "A romantic relationship is ongoing between Bill and Marge." Or "Bill and Marge are currently implementing an interactive romantic relationship." Or still better, "One can easily see that an interactive romantic relationship is currently being fulfilled between Bill and Marge." Ridiculous contrived examples? Here are some real ones.

A businessman denied a loan does not suffer but instead says, "I went through a suffering process." A teacher does not say, "If you use a calculator in class, you will never learn to add and subtract," but instead, "The fact is that the use of the calculator in the classroom is negative for the learning process." An undergraduate wants to say that "Every UCLA freshman needs to learn how to cope with crowds," but it comes out as "There can be little doubt that contending with the problem of overpopulation at UCLA is one thing that every freshman needs to learn how to do." Instead of being invited "to recruit," a corporation is asked "to participate in

1

the recruitment process." A university bureaucrat wants to make a generous offer: "To encourage broadband system use, the ACAD will pay all line charges for the next two years." But instead, it comes out as: "In order to stimulate utilization of the broadband system, it is the intention of the ACAD to provide for central funding of all monthly line charges generated by attachment to the system over the period of the next two years." A politician "indicates his reluctance to accept the terms on which the proposal was offered" when he might have said "No." A teacher of business writing tells us not that "People entering business today must learn to speak effectively," but "One of these factors is the seemingly increasing awareness of the idea that to succeed in business, it is imperative that the young person entering a business career possess definite skill in oral communication."

All these people write, and maybe even think, in the Official Style. The Official Style comes in many dialects— government, military, social scientific, lab scientific, MBA flapdoodle—but all exhibit the same basic attributes. They all build on the same imbalance, a dominance of nouns and an atrophy of verbs. They enshrine the triumph, worshipped in every bureaucracy, of stasis over action. Real actions lurk furtively in each of the sentences I've just quoted—suffer, learn, cope, recruit, pay, speak—but they are swamped by lame "is" verbs, "shun" words ("facilitation," "intention"), and strings of prepositional phrases.

This basic imbalance between action and inertia is easy to cure, if you want to cure it—and this book's Paramedic Method tells you how to do it. *But when do you want to cure it?* We all sometimes feel, whatever setting we write in, that we will be penalized for writing in plain English. It will sound too flip. Unserious. Even satirical. In my academic dialect, that of literary study, writing plain English nowadays is tantamount to walking down the hall naked as a jaybird. Public places demand protective coloration; sometimes you must write in the Official Style. And when you do, how do you make sure you are writing a good Official Style—if there is one—rather than a bad one? What can "good" and "bad" mean when applied to prose in this way?

Revising Prose starts out by teaching you how to revise the Official Style. But after you've learned that, we'll reflect on what such revision is likely to do for you, or to you, in the bureaucratic world of the future—and the future is only going to get more bureaucratic, however many efforts we make to simplify it, and its official language. You ought then to be able to see what "good" and "bad" mean for prose, and what you are doing when you revise it. And that means you will know how to socialize your revisory talents, how to put them, like your sentences, into action.

PREPOSITIONAL-PHRASE STRINGS: SMEARS AND HICCUPS

We can begin with three examples of student prose:

This sentence is in need of an active verb.

Physical satisfaction is the most obvious of the consequences of premarital sex.

In response to the issue of equality for educational and occupational mobility, it is my belief that a system of inequality exists in the school system.

What do they have in common? They have been assembled from strings of prepositional phrases glued together by that all-purpose epoxy "is." In each case the sentence's verbal force has been shunted into a noun, and its verbal force has been diluted into "is," the neutral copulative, the weakest verb in the language. Such sentences project no life, no vigor. They just "are." And the "is" generates those strings of prepositional phrases fore and aft. It's so easy to fix. Look for the real action. Ask yourself, who's kicking who? (Yes, I know, it should be *whom*, but doesn't *whom* sound stilted? In this book, we'll stick with *who*.)

In "This sentence is in need of an active verb," the action obviously lies in "need." And so, "This sentence needs an active verb." The needless prepositional phrase "in need of" simply disappears once we realize who's kicking who. The sentence, animated by a real verb, comes alive, and in six words instead of nine.

Where's the action in "physical satisfaction is the most obvious of the consequences of premarital sex"? Buried down there in "satisfaction." But just asking the question reveals other problems. Satisfaction isn't a consequence of premarital sex, in the same way that, say, pregnancy is. And, as generations of both sexes will attest, sex, premarital or otherwise, does not always satisfy. Beyond all this, the contrast between the clinical phrasing of the sentence, with its lifeless "is" verb, and the life-giving power of lust in action makes the sentence seem almost funny. Excavating the action from "satisfaction" yields "Premarital sex satisfies! Obviously!" This gives us a Lard Factor of 66% and a comedy factor even higher. (You find the Lard Factor by dividing the difference between the number of words in the original and the revision by the number of words in the original. In this case, 12−4 = 8; 8÷12 = 67%. If you've not paid attention to your own writing before, think of a Lard Factor (LF) of one-third to one-half as normal and don't stop revising until you've removed it. The comedy factor in prose revision, though often equally great, does not lend itself to numerical calculation.)

But how else do we revise here? "Premarital sex is fun, obviously" may be a little better, but we remain in thrall to "is." And the frequent falsity of the observation stands out yet more. Revision has exposed the empty thinking. The writer makes it even worse by continuing, "Some degree of physical satisfaction is present in almost all coitus." Add it all together and we get something like, "People usually enjoy premarital sex" (LF 58%). At its worst, academic prose makes us laugh by describing ordinary reality in extraordinary language.

Now for the third example.

> In response to the issue of equality for educational and occupational mobility, it is my belief that a system of gender inequality exists in the school system.

A diagram reveals the problem and points to a lurking action:

> In response
> to the issue
> of equality
> for educational and occupational mobility,
>
> it *is* my belief that a system
>
> of gender inequality exists
> in the school system.

A string of prepositional phrases, then a form of the verb "to be" (usually "is"), then more prepositional phrases. But sandwiched in the middle lurks, furtive and afraid, the real *action* of the sentence: "it is my belief that." Change that from the "is" form to the active voice, and we have *an action*. Somebody *believes* something. Everything before and after this action amounts to a single phrase—"gender inequality." So we have this revision:

> I believe that gender inequality exists in the schools. (9 words instead of 26; LF 65%)

The drill for this problem stands clear. Circle every form of "to be" (*is, was, will be, seems to be, have been*) and every prepositional phrase (*of, in, by, through, from,* etc.). Then find out who's kicking who and start rebuilding the sentence with that action. Two prepositional phrases in a row turn on the warning light, three make a problem, and four demand immediate surgery. Look for the real *action* hidden behind the "is" and prepositional phrases. So here:

Original

The history of new regulatory provisions is that there is generally an immediate resistance to them.

What hides behind "is that there is"? *Resistance.* And behind that? *Resist!* Now we need an *actor.* We have to invent one, but clearly "people in general" are acting here. So:

Revision

People usually resist new regulations.

Five words instead of 16, for a LF of 69%. The two original prepositional phrases have been eliminated. The action—*resist*—stands clear. A little practice in this kind of revision and, instead of writing "There are many ways in which people resist change," you'll say "People resist change in many ways."

The action lies in an even deeper grave of prepositions in this example:

The project is likely to result in a minor population increase in the City from families relocating to the site from outside the community.

Chart first:

The project
is likely
to result
in a minor population increase
in the City
from families relocating
to the site
from outside the community.

The classic Official Style formula: an "is," an infinitive "to" phrase, then five prepositional phrases in a row. For once, we

ACTION

have a clear actor—"The project." We'll start there. What is the project *doing*? What verb would express "a minor population increase from outside the City to inside the City"? How about "attract"? What is being "attracted"? Families. It all falls into place.

Revision

The project will probably attract new families to the city.

Good work: (1) 24 words cut down to 10, for a Lard Factor of 58%; (2) five prepositional phrases and one infinitive phrase shrunk to one prepositional phrase; (3) above all, a clearly defined *action*—"attract."

Sometimes people go to grotesque lengths to hide the action from their readers. Look here at an undergraduate disqualifying him or herself from membership in a creative writing class: "The type of writing that I have an interest in is in the area of creative writing." To get into the class, write instead, "I want to study creative writing" (17 words into 6; LF 66%). Or take this simple example:

Original

There are several examples of this selection process present in the Listerine ad.

Revision

The Listerine ad exemplifies this selection process.

Sometimes potential actions are smeared across the whole sentence. Here's a favorite of mine:

These are disturbed habitats (e.g. roadsides, vacant lots) vegetated by weedy colonizing species which depend on repeated disturbances for their existence.

The Official Style is at its silliest in describing ordinary things like weeds. It just can't stand giving them their plain, ordinary names. A weed has to become "a weedy colonizing species." Now, Where's the Action? Well, we have a choice:

disturb
vegetate
colonize
depend
disturb [again]
exist

Which offers the central action? None of them. There *isn't any* central action. I think—it is a guess—that the central, though unexpressed, *action* amounts to this:

Weeds *grow* faster in empty spaces.

If I have guessed right, we've reduced 21 words to 6, for a LF of 71%. Not bad for government work. Now another Official Style smear job:

Perception is the process of extracting information from stimulation emanating from the objects, places, and events in the world around us.

A diagram helps:

Perception
is the process
of extracting information
from stimulation emanating
from the objects, places, and events
in the world
around us.

Again, look at the possible actions:

perceive
process
extract
inform
stimulate
emanate

Actor is clear, and *action*, too: "Perception extracts information."
The rest of the sentence goes into a single prepositional
phrase: "from the outside world."

Revision

Perception extracts information from the outside world.

Profound? No. Clear? Yes. Instead of 21 words, 7, for a LF
of 66% exactly. And a 5-to-1 prepositional-phrase kill ratio.
Sometimes in revision you want so badly to emphasize the
central action that you ruthlessly cut away some of the sur-
rounding details.

Next, a sentence from an Environmental Impact Statement:

Pelicans may also be vulnerable to direct oiling, but the lack of
mortality data despite numerous spills in areas frequented by the
species suggests that it practices avoidance.

You want to dig out the "avoid" in the Official Style "practices avoidance." And it is clear who is doing the avoiding:
the pelicans. So this:

Revision

Pelicans seem to survive oil spills by avoiding the oil.

Have I left out anything essential in getting from 28 words
to 10 (LF 64%)?

Official Style sentences smother action the way foam puts out a fire. Look at these strings from a lawyer, a scientist, and an historian:

Here is an example *of* the use *of* the rule *of* justice *in* argumentation.

One *of* the most important results *of* the presentation *of* the data is the alteration *of* the status *of* the elements *of* the discourse.

Another index *of* the breadth *of* the dissemination *of* Christian literature *in* this period is the appearance *of* translations *of* Christian scriptural documents *into* a variety *of* provincial languages.

The *of* strings are the worst of all. They seem to reenact a series of hiccups. When you revise them, you can feel how fatally easy the "is" + prepositional-phrase Official Style formula is for prose style. They blur the central action of the sentence—you can't find out what is actually going on. Let's try revising.

Original

Here is an example *of* the use *of* the rule *of* justice *in* argumentation.

"Rule of justice" is a term of art, so we must leave it intact. After we have found an active verb—"exemplify"—buried in "is an example of the use of," the rest follows easily.

Revision

This passage exemplifies argumentation using the rule of justice.

Now, how about the second sentence? It represents a perfectly symmetrical Official Style pattern: string of prepositional phrases + "is" + string of prepositional phrases. Let's diagram it for emphasis:

One

of the most important results

of the presentation
of the data

is the alteration

of the status
of the elements
of the discourse.

Notice the formulaic character? The monotonous rhythm? The blurred action? Try reading it aloud: *of* dadadum, *of* dadadum, *of* dadadum. I'm not sure what this sentence means, but the action must be buried in "alteration." Start there, with an active, transitive verb—"alter." How about "Presentation of the data alters the status of the discourse elements"? Or less formally, "The status of the discourse elements depends on how you present the data." Or it may mean, "You don't know the status of the elements until you have presented the data." At least two different meanings swim beneath the formulaic prose. To revise it you must *rethink* it.

Now, the third sentence. Diagram first:

Another index
of the breadth
of the dissemination
of Christian literature
in this period

is the appearance

of translations
of Christian scriptural documents
into a variety
of provincial languages.

The standard Official Style Sandwich: "is" between two thick layers of prepositional phrases. We know what to do: generate an active, transitive verb, and get rid of those thick slices of prepositional phrases. Now, make no mistake about it; it is *hard* to figure out the central action in this sentence. Let me take a stab at it. First, we'll select an *actor*.

> Translation of Christian scriptures into provincial languages...

Now, what is this "translation" *doing*?

> shows how broadly Christian literature is disseminated...

So how about this:

> Translations into provincial languages show how broadly Christian Scriptures were disseminated in this period.

It is not the greatest revision in the world, but we have cut the sentence length in half, and reduced the prepositional phrases from eight to two. Often in revising an academic Official Style you discover, as here, that the root assertion is blurred and confused.

One more example of action-burial, this one in a shallow grave. A police report goes this way:

> Subject officer attempted to enter his vehicle in order to report for work. He was confronted by a skunk who denied him entrance into his vehicle. An officer-involved shooting occurred, resulting in the demise of the skunk.

"An officer-involved shooting occurred, resulting in the demise of the skunk," instead of "He shot the skunk" shows the Official Style at its fullest and finest.

"BLAH BLAH *IS THAT*" OPENINGS

The formulaic slo-mo opening often provides your first taste of the Official Style. It delays and weakens the main action verb when (or *if*) you get to it. *The fact of the matter is that* we all fall into this habit. Let's look at some typical examples of what we will call the "Blah blah *is that*" opening from students, professors, and writers at large:

What I would like to signal here *is that*...

My contention *is that*...

What I want to make clear *is that*...

What has surprised me the most *is that*...

All that really means *is that*...

The upshot of what Heidegger says here *is that*...

The first *is that*...

The point I wish to make *is that*...

What I have argued here *is that*...

The important fundamental to remember *is that*...

My opinion *is that* on this point we have only two options...

My point *is that* the question of the discourse of the human sciences...

The fact of the matter *is that* the material of this article is drawn directly from...

Finally, the result of the use of all these new techniques and methods *is that*...

The one thing that Belinda does not realize *is that* Dorimant knows exactly how to press her buttons.

Easy to fix this pattern: just amputate the mindless preludial fanfare. Start the sentence with whatever follows "Blah blah *is that*...." Cut to the chase. On a word processor it couldn't be simpler: do a global search for the phrase "is that" and revise it out each time. For example:

The upshot of what **Heidegger says** here is that...

My opinion is that on this point **we have only two options**...

My point is that the question of **the discourse of the human sciences**...

The fact of the matter is that **the material of this article is drawn directly from**...

We can even improve my favorite from this anthology:

> The one thing that **Belinda does not realize** is that **Dorimant knows exactly how to press her buttons.**

By amputating the fanfare, you *start fast*, and a fast start may lead to major motion. That's what we're after. Where's the *action*?

Writers addicted to the "blah blah *is that*" dead rocket oftentimes tie themselves in knots with it. One writes: "The position **we are at is this**." Another: "The traditional opposite notion **to this is that there are**...." And a third, a university professor, in an article accurately titled "On the Weakness of Language in the Human Sciences," offers this spasmodic set of *thises, thats,* and *whats*:

> Now **what** I would like to know specifically **is this: what** is the meaning of **this** "as" **that** Heidegger emphasizes so strongly when he says **that** "**that** which is explicitly understood"—**that is, that** which is interpreted—"has the structure of something as something"? My opinion **is that** what Heidegger means is **that** the structure of interpretation (*Auslegung*) is figural rather than, say, intentional. [Emphasis mine.]

In escaping from this Houdini straightjacket, a couple of mechanical tricks come in handy. Besides eliminating the "is's" and changing every passive voice ("is defended by") to an active voice ("defends"), you can squeeze the compound verbs

14

hard, make every "are able to" into a "can," every "seems to succeed in creating" into "creates," every "cognize the fact that" (no, I didn't make it up) into "think," every "am hopeful that" into "hope," every "provides us with an example of" into "exemplifies," every "seeks to reveal" into "shows," and every "there is the inclusion of" into "includes."

Then, after amputating those mindless *fact that* introductory-phrase fanfares, you'll start fast. After that fast start, "cut to the chase," as they say in the movies, as soon as you can. Instead of "the answer is in the negative," you'll find yourself saying "No."

THE PM

We now have the beginnings of the Paramedic Method (PM):

1. Circle the prepositions.
2. Circle the "is" forms.
3. Ask, "Where's the action?" "Who's kicking who?"
4. Put this "kicking" action in a simple (not compound) active verb.
5. Start fast—no slow windups.

Let's use the PM on a more complex instance of blurred action, the opening sentences of an undergraduate psych paper.

> The history of Western psychological thought has long been dominated by philosophical considerations as to the nature of man. These notions have dictated corresponding considerations of the nature of the child within society, the practices by which children were to be raised, and the purposes of studying the child.

Two actions here—"dominate" and "dictate"—but neither has fully escaped from its native stone. The prepositional-phrase and infinitive strings just drag them down.

The history...
of Western psychological thought...
by philosophical considerations...
as to the nature...
of man...
...
of the nature...
of the child...
within society...
by which children...
to be raised...
of studying...

In asking "Where's the action?" and "Who's kicking who?" we next notice all the actions fermenting in the nouns: *thinking* in "thought," *consider* in "considerations," more *thinking* somewhere in "notions." They hint at actions they don't supply and so blur the actor-action relationship still further. We want, remember, a plain active verb, no prepositional-phrase strings, and a natural actor firmly in charge.

> The **actor** must be: "philosophical considerations as to the nature of man."
>
> The **verb**: "dominates."
>
> The **object** of the action: "the history of Western psychological thought."

Now the real problems emerge. What does "philosophical considerations as to the nature of man" really mean? Buried down there is a question: "What is the nature of man?" The "philosophical considerations" just blur this question rather than narrow it. Likewise, the object of the action—"the history of Western psychological thought"—can be simply "Western psychological thought." Shall we put all this together in the passive form that the writer used?

Western psychological thought has been dominated by a single question: what is the nature of man?

Or, with an active verb:

A single question has dominated Western psychological thought: what is the nature of man?

Our formulaic concern with the stylistic surface—passives, prepositional phrases, kicker and kickee—has led to a much more focused thought.

The first sentence passes its baton awkwardly to the second. "Considerations," confusing enough as we have seen, become "these notions" at the beginning of the second sentence, and these "notions," synonymous with "considerations" in the first sentence, dictate more but different "considerations" in the second. We founder in these vague and vaguely synonymous abstractions. Our unforgiving eye for prepositional phrases then registers "*of* the nature *of* the child *within* society." We don't need "within society"; where else will psychology study children? And "the nature of the child" telescopes to "the child." We metamorphose "the practices by which children were to be raised" into "child-rearing," and "the purposes in studying the child" leads us back to "corresponding considerations of the nature of the child within society," which it partly overlaps. But we have now a definite actor, remember, in the first sentence—the "single question." So a tentative revision:

This basic question leads to three others: What are children like? How should they be raised? Why should we study them?

Other revisions suggest themselves. Work out a couple. In mine, I've used "question" as the baton passed between the two sentences because it clarifies the relationship between the two. And I've tried to expose what real, clear action lay hidden beneath the conceptual cotton-wool of "these notions have dictated corresponding considerations."

Revision

A single question has dominated Western psychological thought: What is the nature of man? This basic question leads to three others. What are children like? How should they be raised? Why should we study them?

A PAUSE FOR REFLECTION

This two-sentence example of student academic prose rewards some reflection. First, the sentences boast no grammatical or syntactical mistakes. Second, they need not have come from a student. Any issue of a psychology journal or text will net you a dozen from the same mold. How else did the student learn to write them? Third, not many instructors reading this prose will think anything is wrong with it. Just the opposite. It reads just right; it sounds *professional*. The teacher's comment on this paper reads, in full: "An excellent paper—well conceived, well organized and well written—A+." Yet a typical specimen sentence from it makes clear neither its main actor nor action; its thought consistently puffs into vague general concepts like "considerations," "notions," and the like; and its cradle-rocking monotonous rhythm puts us to sleep. It reveals a mind writing in formulas, out of focus, above all a mind putting no pressure on itself. The writer is not thinking so much as, on a scale slightly larger than normal, filling in the blanks.

You can't build bridges thinking in this muddled way; they will fall down. If you bemuse yourself thus in a chemistry lab, you'll blow up the apparatus. And yet the student, obviously bright, has been invited to write this way and rewarded for it. He or she has been doing *a stylistic imitation*, and has brought if off successfully. Chances are that the focused, plain-language version I've offered would get a lower grade than the Official Style original. Revision is always perilous and paradoxical, but nowhere more so than in the academic world. Not so perilous, though, as bridges that fall down or lab apparatus that blows up. In the long run, it is better to get your thinking straight and take your chances.

WHEN "IS" IS OK

We've been practicing the first five rules of the PM. Let's put them before us again.

1. Circle the prepositions.
2. Circle the "is" forms.
3. Ask, "Where's the action?" "Who's kicking who?"
4. Put this "kicking" action in a simple (not compound) active verb.
5. Start fast—no slow windups.

At the center of this grouping stands the search for *action*. In the Official Style, action usually comes in only one flavor— "is." We've been revising "is" into transitive, active verbs that impart the breath of life.

But rules don't always work and exceptions exist, if not to disprove them, to encourage common sense in applying them. As a segue to the next chapter, which examines sentence *shapes*, let's look at two passages which take an extreme stand toward "is." The first one uses nothing else. The second abjures it entirely.

First, a passage built on "is." It is from a famous military historian's discussion of the Battle of Agincourt.

Agincourt is one of the most instantly and vividly visualized of all epic passages in English history, and one of the most satisfactory to contemplate. It is a victory of the weak over the strong, of the common soldier over the mounted knight, of resolution over bombast, of the desperate, cornered and far from home, over the proprietorial and cocksure. Visually it is a pre-Raphaelite, perhaps better a Medici Gallery print battle—a composition of strong verticals and horizontals and a conflict of rich dark reds and Lincoln greens against fishscale greys and arctic blues....It is an episode to quicken the interest of any schoolboy ever bored by a history lesson, a set-piece demonstration of English moral superiority and cherished ingredient of a fading national myth. It is also a story of slaughter-yard behavior and of outright atrocity.

The passage is built on a backbone of "is." I've supplied in [boldface brackets] the repetitions only implied by the text.

Agincourt is
    one of the most instantly and vividly visualized of all epic passages in English history, and

    [is] one of the most satisfactory to contemplate.

It is a victory
    of the weak over the strong,
[it is a victory]
    of the common soldier over the mounted knight,
[it is a victory]
    of resolution over bombast,
[it is a victory]
    of the desperate, cornered and far from home, over the proprietorial and cocksure.

Visually it is
    a pre-Raphaelite, perhaps better a Medici Gallery print battle—a composition of strong verticals and horizontals and a conflict of rich dark reds and Lincoln greens against fishscale greys and arctic blues....

It is an episode
    to quicken the interest of any schoolboy ever bored by a history lesson,

ACTION

[it is]
> a set-piece demonstration of English moral superiority and cherished ingredient of a fading national myth.

It is also
> a story of slaughter-yard behavior and of outright atrocity.

Goodness! Everything I've been preaching against! "Is" plus strings of prepositional phrases. But the prose works in this instance because it possesses a shape, a repetitive, chorus-like pattern of similar elements until, in the last sentence, the prose shape remains the same but the sense constitutes a 180-degree inverted climax. Sentence shape matters, and our exploration of the Official Style must consider it.

Now for the opposite extreme, an article from the field of artificial intelligence which makes its point by banishing "to be" completely.

> To devise a new kind of logic we must escape from the old metaphysics. I shall indicate how I have tried to do this. One valuable technique which I recommend, I shall apply in writing this essay. I shall endeavor to write this essay without using the verb "to be." By doing so, I shall subject myself, in an informal way, to an essential discipline which a logic of action should impose, formally, upon its uses. This discipline forces one to think in terms of actions and agents and deprives one of that easy way of begging epistemological questions—the impersonal assertion of truth or existence in the style we normally expect of scientific writers.

No "is"s, but no shape either, just an awkward chorus of "I"s. Again, shape matters. Shape and rhythm. To the remaining rules of the Paramedic Method, those which deal with shape and rhythm, we now turn.

CHAPTER 2

SHAPE

IFYOUDON'TTHINKTHATSHA
PEMATTERSINWHATYOUREA
DTRYREADINGTHISANDS
EEIFYOUDONTMISSTHECLU
ESWHICHVISUALSPACINGUS
UALLYPROVIDES. THISISHO
WTEXTAPPEAREDFORMUC
HOFWESTERNWRITINGHIS
TORY.

Scribes didn't start leaving spaces between words until sometime in the eighth century A.D. Before that, no separation between words or sentences, and usually no punctuation or capitalization, either. The eye could render no aid to the comprehending mind. When spaces divide words from one another, the words have enough free space on either side so that they can have a shape. We are free to consider the shape of the words. And we do. We read, when we are reading for rapid comprehension, partly by the shape of the word.

Text was crowded together unspaced partly because writing, and writing surfaces, cost a great deal. The electronic screen makes white space free and so frees us to think of sentences as shapes. In the world of print, sentence shape has always been important. On the digital screen, it becomes even more so. This importance is already feeding back onto printed text, making us look at sentences as visual constructions. Shape matters. In this chapter, we'll examine how it matters, and explore how the Official Style's characteristic *shapelessness* makes it so hard to read. Shape leads to voice, which we will consider in the chapter following this one.

The first five rules of the Paramedic Method all aim at *action*. Here they are again.

1. Circle the prepositions.
2. Circle the "is" forms.
3. Ask, "Where's the *action*?" "Who's kicking who?"
4. Put this central action in a simple active verb.
5. Start fast—no slow windups.

When we put these rules to work in the previous chapter, we unearthed a characteristic *shape* for Official Style sentences. It looked like a freight train with the engine—a small engine—in the middle.

Prep. phrase + prep. phrase + prep. phrase + IS + prep. phrase + prep. phrase + prep. phrase.

You remember how they go: "Thus the first step **in** establishing the basis **of** the study **of** semiotics **in** relation **to** writing and typography **IS** blah blah blah."

LOOK SHARP

The last three rules of the Paramedic Method address sentence shape directly. Like the first five, they are simple and require no technical expertise.

6. Write out each sentence on a blank screen or sheet of paper and mark off its basic rhythmic units with a "/".
7. Mark off sentence lengths in the passage with a big "/" between sentences.
8. Read the passage aloud with emphasis and feeling.

In our revisions, we can't ignore the first five, but we'll think about them from a visual point of view.

Let's begin with two extreme examples to get us thinking. The first comes from one of the great pitchers for the old Brooklyn Dodgers (back when the Dodgers were in Brooklyn), Preacher Roe. One day he was knocked out of the box in the second inning. A reporter, asking the kind of intrusive question reporters love to ask, asked him how it felt to be knocked out so early in the game. Old Preach replied, with sense and dignity: "Well, sometimes you eat the bear and sometimes the bear eats you." You could hardly ask for a more visual depiction of fortune—now on your side, now against you. This pattern of writing was called *chiasmus* by the classical Greek rhetoricians because its reversal looked like a Greek "Chi," or "X."

Sometimes you eat the bear

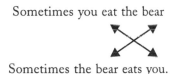

Sometimes the bear eats you.

The shape of the sentence creates and embodies its sense.

Chiasmus works so well that writers have used it in many different situations. President John F. Kennedy, in his inaugural address, urged his countrymen: "Ask not what **your country** can do for *you*, but what *you* can do for **your country**." Samuel Johnson, the great eighteenth-century lexicographer, responded to an aspiring author with these words: "Your manuscript is both good and original; but the part that is **good** is not *original*, and the part that is *original* is not **good**." David Gardner, a past president of the University of

California, said in exasperation to a faculty assembly consid-
ering ethnic balance in the university: "Anyone who thinks he
has a solution does not *comprehend the problem* and anyone
who *comprehends the problem* **does not have a solution.**"
The pattern works in many contexts because the eye helps
the mind see the sentence as a simple pattern. There is no
great mystery to a visual aid like this. Anyone can do it. Let
me give you an example of another kind—parallelism—from
today's newspaper. Every year, Castroville, California, the
"artichoke capital of the world," puts on, as you might expect,
an artichoke festival. Last year, however, El Niño washed it
out. The manager of the California Artichoke Advisory Board
explained it in a wonderfully shaped phrase: "Artichokes can
stand a little water, but they can't swim." Bingo! Short, quick,
emphatic, memorable. A perfect sound bite. If she had been
a typical Official Style bureaucrat, she would have said: "Due
to the incidence of unprecedented amounts of rainfall occa-
sioned by the El Niño phenomenon, the artichoke crop, which
can usually be depended upon to withstand the impact of the
traditional levels of rainfall commonly experienced in the
artichoke-growing process, has been very significantly im-
pacted in volume and amount, to such a degree as to make it
impractical to implement or facilitate the annual Artichoke
Festival." Or something like that.

In some kinds of writing, though, the eye is statutorily
banished—legal writing, for example. Figure 1 presents a sentence from Section 470 (Forgery) of the California Penal
Code. I've enlarged and enhanced the subject and verb, so that
you can connect them in your eye; no ordinary reader could
ever put them together. By the time we get to the end of this
endless sentence, we're totally lost.

What would such an intimidating document look like if
we tried to *help* the eye rather than *hinder* it? Figure 2 tries
to do this. It separates (or tries—I'm not a lawyer and some
of the sub-sub-subdependencies are ambiguously referential)
the main argument from the many qualifications and lists of
particular offenses. The language of the law proceeds always

Every person

who, with intent to defraud, signs the name of another person, or
a fictitious person, knowing that he or she has no authority so to
do, or falsely makes, alters, forges or counterfeits, any charter,
letters patent, deed, lease, indenture, writing obligatory, will,
testament, codicil, bond, covenant, bank bill or note, post note,
check, draft, bill of exchange, contract, promissory note, due bill
for the payment of money or property, receipt for money or
property, passage ticket, lottery ticket or share purporting to be
issued under the California State Lottery Act of 1984, trading
stamp, power of attorney, certificate of ownership or other document evidencing ownership of a vehicle or undocumented vessel,
or any certificate of any share, right, or interest in the stock of any
corporation or association, or any controller's warrant for the
payment of money at the treasury, county order or warrant, or
request for the payment of money, or the delivery of goods or
chattels or any kind, or for the delivery of any instrument of
writing, or acquittance, release, or receipt for money or goods, or
any acquittance, release, or discharge of any debt, account, suit,
action, demand, or other thing, real or personal, or any transfer or
assurance of money, certificate of shares of stock, goods, chattels,
or other property whatever, or any letter of attorney, or other
power to receive money, or to receive or transfer certificates of
shares of stock or annuities, or to let, lease, dispose of, alien, or
convey any goods, chattels, lands, or tenements, or other estate,
real or personal, or any acceptance or endorsement of any bill of
exchange, promissory note, draft, order, or an assignment of any
bond, writing obligatory, promissory note, or other contract for
money or other property; or counterfeits or forges the seal or
handwriting of another; or utters, publishes, passes, or attempts to
pass, as true and genuine, any of the above-named false, altered,
forged, or counterfeited matters, as above specified and described,
knowing the same to be false, altered, forged, or counterfeited,
with intent to prejudice, damage, or defraud any person; or who,
with intent to defraud, alters, corrupts, or falsifies any record of
any will, codicil, conveyance, or other instrument, the record of
which is by law evidence, or any record of any judgment of a court
or the return of any officer to any process of any court

is guilty of forgery.

Figure 1

𝔈𝔟𝔢𝔯𝔶 𝔭𝔢𝔯𝔰𝔬𝔫
𝔴𝔥𝔬,
with intent to defraud,
𝔰𝔦𝔤𝔫𝔰 𝔱𝔥𝔢 𝔫𝔞𝔪𝔢 𝔬𝔣 𝔞𝔫𝔬𝔱𝔥𝔢𝔯 𝔭𝔢𝔯𝔰𝔬𝔫,
or a fictitious person,

knowing that he or she has no authority so to do,

𝔬𝔯 𝔣𝔞𝔩𝔰𝔢𝔩𝔶 𝔪𝔞𝔨𝔢𝔰,
𝔞𝔩𝔱𝔢𝔯𝔰,
𝔣𝔬𝔯𝔤𝔢𝔰 𝔬𝔯 𝔠𝔬𝔲𝔫𝔱𝔢𝔯𝔣𝔢𝔦𝔱𝔰,
any charter,
letters patent,
deed,
lease,
indenture,
writing obligatory,
will,
testament,
codicil,
bond,
covenant,
bank bill or note,
post note,
check,
draft,
bill of exchange,
contract,
promissory note,
due bill for the payment of money or property,
receipt for money or property,
passage ticket,
lottery ticket
> or share purporting to be issued under the California State Lottery Act of 1984,

trading stamp,
power of attorney,
certificate of ownership
> or other document evidencing ownership of a vehicle or undocumented vessel,

Figure 2

Error

 ---

or any certificate
> of any share, right, or interest in the stock of any corporation or association,

or any controller's warrant
> for the payment of money at the treasury,

county order
or warrant,
or request
> for the payment of money,
> or the delivery of goods or chattels or any kind,
> or for the delivery of any instrument of writing,

or acquittance,
[or] release,
or receipt for money or goods,
or any acquittance,
release,
or discharge of any
> debt,
> account,
> suit,
> action,
> demand,
> or other thing, real or personal,

or any transfer
or assurance of
> money,
> certificate of shares of stock,
> goods,
> chattels,
> or other property whatever,

or any letter of attorney,
or other power
> to receive money,
> or to receive or transfer
>> certificates of shares of stock or annuities,

> or to let,
>> lease,
>>> dispose of,
>>>> alien,
>>>>> or convey
>> any goods,

Figure 2 (continued)

chattels,
lands,
or tenements,
or other estate, real or personal,

or any acceptance or endorsement of any
bill of exchange,
promissory note,
draft,
order,
or an assignment of any
bond,
writing obligatory,
promissory note,
or other contract
for money or other property;

or counterfeits or forges
the seal or handwriting of another;
or utters,
publishes,
passes,
or attempts to pass,
as true and genuine,
any of the above-named
false,
altered,
forged,
or counterfeited
matters,
as above specified and described,

knowing the same to be
with intent to prejudice,
damage, or
defraud
any person;

Figure 2 (continued)

30

or who,
with intent to defraud,
alters,
corrupts,
or falsifies
  any record
    of any will,
    codicil,
    conveyance,
    or other instrument,
        the record of which is by law evidence,
  or any record
    of any judgment of a court
      or the return
      of any officer
      to any process
      of any court

is guilty of forgery.

Figure 2 (continued)

from an *iterative* strategy: it tries to iterate every possible case, rather than grouping them under a generalizing metaphor. This strategy, supposed to preclude argument, usually works in the opposite direction. In revising it—and plain-language laws now mandate this in some cases—some metaphorical compression is usually sought, but only a lawyer can tell which might work. The "visual revision" I've done in figure 2 tries, without altering the words, to give them a *shape* that encourages comprehension. *Anyone* ought to be able to make sense of a complex document in this way. If not, it doesn't make any sense.

Let's try this technique out on another seemingly opaque document, a passage from the *Federal Insecticide, Fungicide, and Rodenticide Act*, printed first in normal typography and lineation.

> Except as otherwise provided in subparagraph (D) (i) of this paragraph, with respect to data submitted after December 31, 1969, by an applicant or registrant to support an application for registration, experimental use permit, or amendment adding a new use to an existing registration, to support or maintain in effect an existing registration, or for reregistration, the Administrator may, without the permission of the original data submitter, consider any such item of data in support of an application by any other person (hereinafter in this subparagraph referred to as the "applicant") within the fifteen-year period following the date the data were originally submitted only if the applicant has made an offer to compensate the original data submitter and submitted such offer to the Administrator accompanied by evidence of delivery to the original data submitter of the offer.

Confusin', ain't it? But all of us, in one way or another, must cope with such government regulations. Suppose you *must*, first, *understand*, the passage, and then, two, if possible revise it. Diagraming can help the eye to detect the *underlying shape* of the passage. Figure 3 illustrates how a student of mine reformatted the sentence to foreground the basic *shape* of the sentence. (And it is all *one sentence*.) To *revise* this sentence, I think you would have to know something about pesticides, and I don't, so I shan't try. But if I had to, I would at least know where to start: "The administrator may consider…," etc.

If you want to know how complex regulations like the two previous ones will appear when thoroughly acclimated to the digital space of the computer screen, imagine the two diagrams as occurring in a *three-dimensional* expressive field, with the various type sizes denoting distances from the top of the space. The reader would *fly into* this space, starting with the shape of the sentence's fundamental utterance and then penetrating

Except as otherwise provided in subparagraph (D) (i) of this paragraph,
with respect to data submitted after December 31, 1961,
    by <u>an applicant</u>
    or <u>registrant</u>
        to support an application for   *registration,*
                                experimental use permit,
                  or *amendment*
                        adding a new use to an existing registration
                        to support or maintain in effect an existing registration
                              or for reregistration,

the Administrator may
without the permission of the original data submitter,
    consider any such item of data
      in support of an application
        by any other person
            (hereinafter in this subparagraph referred to as the "applicant")
        within the fifteen-year period following the date the data were
        originally submitted
    only if the applicant <u>has made</u> an offer to compensate
    the original data submitter
      and <u>submitted</u> such offer to the Administrator
        accompanied by evidence of delivery to the original data
        submitter of the offer.

Figure 3

down to the various levels of qualification. The text would
have a three-dimensional shape.

SHOPPING BAGS AND CLUNKERS

The Official Style, as we've seen, builds its sentences on a form
of the verb "to be" plus strings of prepositional phrases fore
and aft; it buries the action of its verbs in nominative constructions with the passive voice; it often separates the natural subject from the natural verb, actor from action, by big

chunks of verbal sludge; it cherishes the long windup and the slo-mo opening. Add all these attributes together and you have a sentence which has no natural shape to express its meaning. Instead, you get something like a shopping bag that the writer stuffs with words, using the generative formulas we have chronicled. This shapelessness makes them unreadable; read one of them aloud with gusto and emphasis and you'll give yourself the giggles. Try it with the "Forgery" statute. Or with the following Official Style sentence by—of all people—a writing teacher. Try reading it aloud.

> One of the factors that limits and warps the development of a theory of composition and style by teachers of the subject is the tendency to start with failed or inadequate writing and to project goodness as the opposite of badness.

Rule 8, reading prose aloud—not speed-mumbling it but reading it with an actor's care—can tell you a lot about sentence shape. This typical Official Style sentence has no shape which the voice can use to underline the sense. Clunk, clunk, clunk— huh? Factors that limit and warp the *what*? Nothing in the sentence's shape tells you who the natural subject is—writing teachers—or what that subject is *doing*, where the *action* is. Possible subjects there are aplenty:

factors
development
theory
composition
style
teachers
subject

And incipient actions too:

limiting
warping

developing
tending
starting
failing
projecting

But nothing in the sentence's *shape* narrows down our choice among the cornucopia of possible actors and actions.

And if, following Rule 6, you break down each part into the individual freight cars, they seem about equal, and equally unemphatic, as well.

One of the factors/
that limits and warps/
the development of a theory/
of composition and style/

the tendency/
by teachers of the subject /
to start with failed or inadequate writing/
and to project goodness/
as the opposite of badness.

Rule 6 provides a quick glimpse of a sentence's shape. Take your sentence and write it by itself on a computer screen or sheet of paper. Take the process a step further. Sketch its architecture, to chart its lines of force. Break it down into component elements by repeated indentation, as we've done with the legal examples just considered. Try even to draw abstract shapes that reflect its meaning. *Look at its shape.* If you are working on a word-processing program that permits it, box the selection to further frame your attention. You may be able to make the passage easier to understand even before you revise it. I've illustrated this simple technique in figure 4, which depicts our familiar freight train of phrases fore-and-aft, with a small "is" engine pushing from the middle.

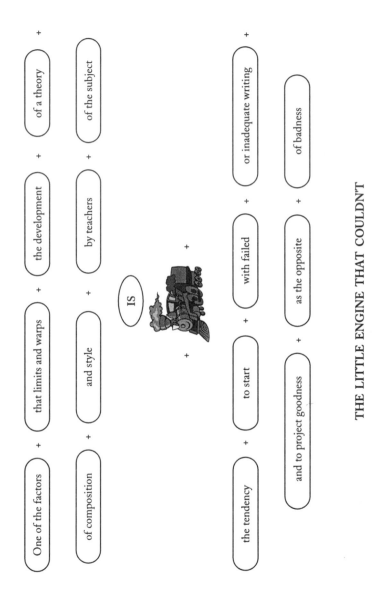

One of the factors + that limits and warps + the development + of a theory +

of composition + and style + by teachers + of the subject +

IS

+

+

+

the tendency + to start + with failed + or inadequate writing +

and to project goodness + as the opposite + of badness

THE LITTLE ENGINE THAT COULDN'T

Figure 4

Now let's visualize an altogether simpler example.

Additional detailed information will be required by the Commission for decisions on projects not specifically described and analyzed in the document.

Start with our usual chart generated by Rules 1–3, plus the slasher operation of Rule 6:

Additional detailed
information/
will be required/
by the Commission/
for decisions on projects/
not specifically described and analyzed/
in the document./

OK. Now let's circle the possible actions.

Additional detailed information/
will be (required/)
by the Commission/
for (decisions) on projects/
not specifically (described) and
(analyzed/)
in the document./

No shape; action buried somewhere in "required" or "decisions" or "described" or "analyzed." Let's try another simple device—rearranging the order of the segments:

by the Commission/
will be required/
Additional detailed information/
for decisions on projects/
not specifically described and analyzed/
in the document./

We can begin to glimpse a shape. Actor? Easy—the Commission. From the passive "will be required" we pluck (Rule 3) the active, transitive verb "need."

The Commission **will need**...

What they need is now clear:

more information

What they will do with it, equally clear:

to vote

Revision

The Commission will need more information to vote on projects not analyzed in the report.

Subject-verb-object lined up in a row, with an explanatory infinitive phrase following—a natural good shape. The Lard Factor is only 29% (on the other hand, suppose you got "only" a 29% raise) but that isn't the crucial issue. Shape is what we needed and shape is what we got.

A favorite Official Style habit is to postpone the action until the end of the sentence, when the sentence itself is about to die of starvation. Let's try another typographical ploy to illustrate how shape goes wrong in a sentence.

The manner in which behavior first shown in a conflict situation may become fixed so that it persists after the conflict has passed is then discussed.

The manner (monstrous malarkey) is discussed.

No actor is given by "is discussed," so we'll invent one, our old English professor, Dormitive H. Guffbag. "Prof. Guffbag then discusses how behavior which first emerges in conflict persists after the conflict has passed." First the actor, then the action, then two balanced and parallel elements:

> Prof. Guffbag then discusses
> how behavior <u>which first emerges in conflict</u>
> <u>persists after the conflict has passed.</u>

The balance and parallel in "emerges–conflict" and "persists–conflict" glue the two elements together. The sentence begins fast, then leads us to a garden whose simple design we can easily comprehend. And the Lard Factor, even after we've added Guffbag-the-actor, 17 instead of 26: LF 35%. Not too shabby. (In case you've forgotten, you compute the Lard Factor by dividing the difference between the number of words in the original and the revision by the number of words in the original. Computing the LF is easy now: most word processors have word-count features and built-in calculators.)

Sometimes you have to rewrite a sentence completely to give it some shape.

> Formal education is the tool best used to increase workers' ability for success.

Sometimes, as here, an awful lot can be wrong with a single sentence. But for a start, let's do a Rule 6:

> Formal education/is the tool/best used/to increase/workers' ability/ for success.

You could, so bland and shapeless runs this sequence, slash after every word. But what about Rules 2 and 3? "Is" doesn't provide the natural action; that obviously lurks in "increase." "Ability for success" is an vague lurch toward a precise meaning we might call "a better job." Let me visualize what happens to sentence shape when we read this sentence.

> **Formal education is the tool** best used ◆□ ⅄■🝆□🝆♋◆🝆 ◆□□&🝆□◆⊠ ♋♌⅄●⅄◆☒ for success.

Formal education has *something* to do with success. So, for some shape and emphasis:

> Formal education gets you a better job.

Or,

> Formal education increases your earning power.

But another meaning floats underneath this one, and confuses things, as I've tried to visualize. "Formal education...is best used...for success." In other words, you *could* use it just to enjoy yourself, but that would be a mistake. You *should* use it to make more dough. We should factor this meaning out into a separate sentence, and construct the two in parallel.

> Formal education gets you a better job.
> It also makes life more fun.

Or maybe, for a real shape:

> Formal education gets you a better job—and maybe a better life.

A Pause for Reflection

Let's pause to reflect on this simple example. The arguments advanced, especially the first one, make easy sense. In ordinary conversation, anyone would say, "Formal education gets you a better job." Why would someone *write* the shapeless Official Style version, "Formal education/is the tool/best used/to increase/workers' ability/for success"? *Training*. No one would naturally write this way. The writer is imitating a dominant style, trying to sound the way a writer should sound, trying to be *pious* and *correct*. The writer is not *making a mistake* so much as putting good energy to bad use.

SHAPE

A POLISH SAUSAGE IN THE SAME STYLE

Now a monster—a Polish sausage of a sentence—by a well-known sociologist. Anyone studying the social sciences, or living in the bureaucratic worlds they dominate, will have to read acres of such prose. Though much more complicated and highfalutin' than the previous example, it aims at the same thing—wearing the right clothes.

> The fact that all selves are constituted by or in terms of the social process, and are individual reflections of it—or rather of this organized behavior pattern which it exhibits, and which they comprehend in their respective structures—is not in the least incompatible with or destructive of the fact that every individual self has its own peculiar individuality, its unique pattern; because each individual within that process, while it reflects in its organized structure the behavior patterns of that process as a whole, does so from its own particular and unique standpoint within that process, and thus reflects in its organized structure a different aspect or perspective of this whole social behavior pattern from that which is reflected in the organized structure of any other individual self within that process (just as every monad in the Leibnizian universe mirrors that universe from a different point of view, and thus mirrors a different aspect or perspective of that universe)

No intentional villainy, then, but merciful heavens, what a hall of "mirrors"! Now, no definition of a sentence really defines much, but every sentence ought somehow to organize a pattern of thought, even if it does not always reduce that thought to bite-sized pieces. This sentence melts down its thoughts as soon as it tries to express them. The arguments *have no shape*. What does it *feel like* when you try to understand this sentence? Let me narrate a "reader's puzzlement" of it.

> **The fact that all selves are constituted by or in terms of the social process,**

41

[Wait a minute: does the "or" imply an opposition? A self constituted by the social process stands opposite to one constituted "in terms of" the social process?]

and are individual reflections of it

[Already we have to grope backwards to see what goes with "and." Ah, I think it is "all selves"; OK, "all selves are individual reflections of the social process"...]

—or rather of this organized behavior pattern which it exhibits,

["this organized behavior pattern"—*what* organized behavior pattern?? Does it = "social process"?—and does "the social process" simply mean "society"? "It" seems to = "the social process," so "the social process" exhibits "<u>this</u> organized behavior pattern"—but what does the "this" refer back to? There is no referent that makes sense...]

and which they comprehend in their respective structures—

[What does the "and" connect back to? Must be "this organized behavior pattern." OK. No, it must refer back to "all selves," since it is plural. So "all selves" comprehend something. Now, what does the "which" refer to? Ah, the "organized behavior pattern," which = "the social process," which = (I think) "society." So, maybe, "all selves are constituted by society and constitute it"? No, ...]

is not in the least incompatible with or destructive of

[Ah, ah! A *verb*—finally!—if only "is"...]

the fact that

[Ah—here is the second assertion, or dead-rocket opening, to go with the first one, with which the passage began...]

42

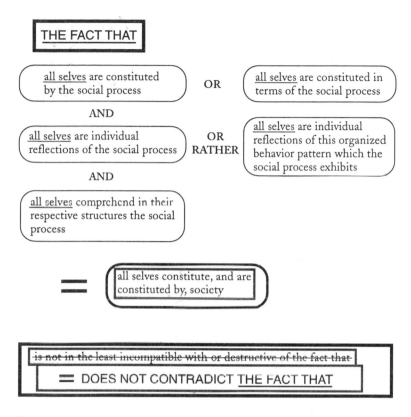

THE FACT THAT

(all selves are constituted by the social process) OR (all selves are constituted in terms of the social process)

AND

(all selves are individual reflections of the social process) OR RATHER (all selves are individual reflections of this organized behavior pattern which the social process exhibits)

AND

(all selves comprehend in their respective structures the social process)

= (all selves constitute, and are constituted by, society)

is not in the least incompatible with or destructive of the fact that

= DOES NOT CONTRADICT THE FACT THAT

Figure 5

At this point, I'm going to give up, for my head is swimming. I'm going, instead, to divide the passage *visually* into separate utterances. The primary problem is *shape*: how do the various utterances—all of them qualified, retracted, doubled back on themselves—relate to one another? The reader's mind desperately needs help from the eye. I do this in figures 5 and 6. Once we've isolated the individual utterances, we'll reconstruct the systemic confusions of the passage, which all stem from how the individual utterances relate to one another. As I hope the diagrams reveal, this passage embodies not prose inelegant

is not in the least incompatible with or destructive of the fact that
= DOES NOT CONTRADICT THE FACT THAT

---

every ~~individual~~ self has its own ~~peculiar~~ individuality, ~~its unique pattern;~~ because each individual within ~~that process,~~ [society] ~~while it~~ reflects ~~in its organized structure~~ the behavior patterns of ~~that process~~ [society] ~~as a whole, does so~~ from its own ~~particular and unique~~ standpoint ~~within that process,~~ and thus reflects ~~in its organized structure~~ a different aspect ~~or perspective~~ of ~~this whole social behavior pattern~~ [society] from that ~~which is~~ reflected ~~in the organized structure of any other individual self within that process~~ [by other selves] (just as every monad in the Leibnizian universe mirrors that universe from [its own] ~~a different~~ point of view, ~~and thus mirrors a different aspect or perspective of that universe~~).

WHICH EQUALS

every self has its own individuality because each individual reflects the behavior patterns of society from its own standpoint, and thus reflects a different aspect of society from that reflected by other selves (just as every monad in the Liebnizian universe mirrors that universe from its own point of view).

SO THE WHOLE SENTENCE AMOUNTS TO

The fact that all selves constitute, and are constituted by, society does not contradict the fact that every self has its own individuality. Each individual reflects society from its own standpoint, and thus reflects a different society from any other self (just as every monad in the Liebnizian universe mirrors that universe from its own point of view).

Figure 6

but prose diseased. Words have proliferated like cancer cells until they have killed the simple meaning they have tried to express. Let's look again at the original and revision. I've pared the revision down to the basic meaning, with all the confusing qualifications and elucidations omitted.

Original

The fact that all selves are constituted by or in terms of the social process, and are individual reflections of it—or rather of this organized behavior pattern which it exhibits, and which they comprehend in their respective structures—is not in the least incompatible with or destructive of the fact that every individual self has its own peculiar individuality, its unique pattern; because each individual within that process, while it reflects in its organized structure the behavior patterns of that process as a whole, does so from its own particular and unique standpoint within that process, and thus reflects in its organized structure a different aspect or perspective of this whole social behavior pattern from that which is reflected in the organized structure of any other individual self within that process (just as every monad in the Leibnizian universe mirrors that universe from a different point of view, and thus mirrors a different aspect or perspective of that universe). (158 words)

Revision

That all selves constitute, and are constituted by, society does not contradict the fact that every self has its own individuality. Each individual reflects society from its own standpoint, and thus reflects a different society from any other self. (39 words)

The argument possesses a symmetry, a *shape*—selves constitute society; society constitutes selves—that I've tried to suggest in the revision. From 158 words, we have distilled 39. A Lard Factor of 75%. But if it takes us three times as long to read the original as the revision, it takes ten times as long to understand it. We can, in fact, understand it *only by revising it*. We should bear this lesson in mind. With practice in *revising prose* comes, always, *practice in reading prose*. We can apply what we have learned in revision even when we are not revising. Practice in revising prose is practice in seeing it. And in *seeing through it*, because we often find, as in this case, a banal truism masquerading as original and profound learning. Practice in revising prose becomes, when pursued to the bitter end, practice in *making clear that you have understood what you have read*. Practice in revising = practice in thinking straight.

NATURAL SHAPES AND BIG MISTAKES

Looking for the natural shape of a sentence often suggests the quickest way to revision. Consider this example:

> I think that all I can usefully say on this point is that in the normal course of their professional activities social anthropologists are usually concerned with the third of these alternatives, while the other two levels are treated as raw data for analysis.

The action starts with "are usually concerned with." Beginning to build a shape means starting here. "Usually, social anthropologists concentrate on the third alternative." Get rid of the triple-padded, pure-babble, dead-rocket opening: "I think that all I can usefully say on this point **is that**...."

~~I think that all I can usefully say on this point is that~~ in the normal course of their professional activities...

"In the normal course of their professional activities" = "usually," and the rest is guff. So: "Usually, social anthropologists concentrate on the third alternative and treat the other two as raw data" ("for analysis" being implied by "raw data"). A final polishing moves "usually" to the other side of "social anthropologists" so as to modify "concentrate" more immediately. The sentence then begins strongly, subject–short modifier–verb, and offers two other emphasis points, "third alternative" and "raw data." And shouldn't we subordinate the "treat" by turning it into a participle? The final revision would then read:

Original

I think that all I can usefully say on this point is that in the normal course of their professional activities social anthropologists are usually concerned with the third of these alternatives, while the other two levels are treated as raw data for analysis.

Revision

Social anthropologists usually concentrate on the third alternative, treating the other two as raw data.

Read it aloud now and then go back to the original and compare (15 words instead of 44; LF 66%). The original is confused and confusing. Two-thirds longer than it should be.

Another pause for reflection. A 66% mistake in this example; 75% in the previous one. What would mistakes of this magnitude look like in another area of human endeavor? A builder who needs three yards of concrete and orders nine? A physician who mistakes the drug and triples the dose? An engineer who calculates a bridge-truss stress at one-third its real level? *Big* mistakes! American college students—indeed, Americans doing all kinds of work after they have finished school—are asked to read a steady diet of this prose, often nothing but. Two lessons, at least, are taught by it: first, often a reader can't understand the assignment, at least not *really*, so just skims it; second, readers, therefore, *need not really pay attention to the words*. Words on a page do not *mean things explicitly*. They only point to generalized meanings in vague formulas.

And so a student writes:

> The most important thing to remember is the fact that interest in the arts has not declined in popularity. (19 words)

instead of

> Interest in the arts has not declined. (7 words; LF 63%)

Or:

> The generation of television is a feeble one, it is a generation lacking in many areas, especially that of artistic background and interest. (23 words)

We don't know whether it is television that is being generated, or an age-group being generated by it. And who knows what "artistic background and interest" means, or what the "many areas" might be. So revision becomes—as so often with the Official Style—both a guess and a satire:

> The TV generation has shown little interest in art—or in anything else either. (14 words; LF 39%)

This sentence shows not bad writing so much as a listless imitation of the vague, approximative prose common in Official Style writing of all sorts.

Shape disciplines thought; shapelessness blurs it. Look at this sentence:

> Heartfelt House has earned a reputation *for* excellence *for* the sharing *of* the wisdom *of* the path *of* compassionate service *in* the natural healing arts.

Or, diagrammatically:

> Heartfelt House has earned a reputation
> *for* excellence

for the sharing
of the wisdom
of the path
of compassionate service
in the natural healing arts.

It does have a shape, to be sure—a laundry list! But ponder the damage that laundry list does to what might otherwise have been a thought. What is Heartfelt House good at? Excellence? Sharing? Wisdom? Path? Compassionate service? Healing arts? Does it all add up to: "Heartfelt House has a good reputation as a nursing home" (LF 60%)? Or is it good at *sharing wisdom*, or *teaching*, or what? No telling. The shape-lessness points to vague, muddled, approximate thinking and, worse, to a *contentment* with such thinking. That is all writing can be expected to express. The Official Style degrades *reading* as well as writing.

What about this sentence?

Throughout our lives, we are exposed to a lot of different teachings and one of them, in our society, is the value placed upon a life in which we are successful.

PM Rule 6:

Throughout our lives,/
we are exposed/
to a lot of different teachings/
and one of them,/
in our society,/
is the value/
placed upon a life/
in which we are successful.

All the shape of a rock-band drum track: *da dum da dum da dum. Actor* and *action* totally disguised. Six preposi-tional phrases. PM Rule 3: Where's the action? Hidden in "teachings." Where's the actor? Buried in "society"! What does "society" "teach"? The "success" hidden in "successful." And so:

Our society teaches the value of success. (LF 77%)

The rest is just floor-shavings, left after the thought has been turned on the lathe. But the Official Style always *includes* the floor-shavings, feels undressed without them, and so this prose does too.

When you cherish the floor-shavings of thought, you spell out the shapeless obvious. You want to say, "On our big campus, you meet many strangers but few friends." But the Official Style version includes all the floor-shavings:

One may encounter many different people on this campus, yet one is rarely recognized as a friend or acquaintance by others and, as a matter of fact, one is more often than not simply ignored or treated as a stranger by those around him or her.

The plain-language version realizes a great savings (76 words instead of 11; LF 76%), but yet more important, it has a natural shape of contrasts that reinforces the sense: *many strangers* v. *few friends.*

Yet again: the Official Style does not come naturally. You have to learn it. And with it comes a habit of reading. Shapeless shopping-bag sentences display more than shapeless verbal jumbles, maddening verbosity, and the floor-shavings of muddled thoughts. An entire way of reading and thinking stands revealed; vague, unfocused, built on temporary generalities themselves built on hopelessly cluttered heaps of general terms, often ending in Latinate *-ion* "shun" words. Such prose asks to be read in a certain way—quickly, inattentively, just for the general drift and the fugitive generalization. It has become the Official Style for pseudo-profundity, pretentious hokum, and pure guff—as we have seen and seen and seen.

THE HUMAN/AIRPLANE INTERFACE

Let me close this chapter with a stylistic comparison. Here are two passages about the relation between airplanes and human beings. The first one tells us how hard it is to measure the pain airplane noise inflicts on people.

> A singular quantitative classification of the individual human response to any given noise level from a particular noise source is not available by virtue of the human quality of the response.

A perfect formulaic, freight-train Official Style sentence, with the little "is" engine pushing ineffectually from the middle:

A singular quantitative classification
   of the individual human response
   to any given noise level
   from a particular noise source

is not available

   by virtue
   of the human quality
   of the response.

The Official Style strives to abolish people as well as their actions. We must resynthesize them. From "individual human response" and "human quality of the response" we get **People.** From "any given noise level" and "particular noise source" we get **sounds.** So we have:

People hear sounds differently.

Passing by without comment the writer's embarrassing confusion of "singular" and "single," we can complete the utterance

with "No single measurement works." And put the two together in a causal relationship:

> Because people hear differently, no single measurement of sound
> works. (LF 68%)

But "works" sounds too abrupt. Maybe we can't avoid "is
possible."

> Because people hear differently, no single measurement of sound
> is possible.

Put the actor and the action into natural alignment, and everything else falls into place. The Official Style abolishes people
and their actions; revision must always resurrect them.

Now, for relief, a description of the human-airplane interface (as an Official Stylist might put it) which has some
shape, and hence some life. It was written by Ian Fleming,
who, the silly James Bond movies have made us forget, was a
considerable prose stylist.

> No, when the stresses are too great for the tired metal, when the
> ground-mechanic who checks the de-icing equipment is crossed
> in love and skimps his job, way back in London, Idlewild, Gan-
> der, Montreal; when those or many things happen, then the little
> warm room with propellers in front falls straight down out of the
> sky into the sea or onto the land, heavier than air, fallible, vain.
> (Ian Fleming, *Live and Let Die*, pp. 150-151)

Let me diagram and highlight the shape, so that you can see
it:

> Now,
> **when** the stresses are too great for the tired metal,
> **when** the ground-mechanic who checks the de-icing equipment
>   is *crossed in love*
>   and *skimps his job*,

way back in London,
Idlewild,
Gander,
Montreal;
when those or many things happen,

then the little warm room with propellers in front
falls straight down
out of the sky
into the sea or
onto the land,

heavier than air,
fallible,
vain.

Try reading this sentence, using the diagramed version as a
text. Don't be afraid to add rests between prose measures, to
use the pitch of your voice to underline the natural shapes of
the individual phrases. Try it. Notice how the string of prepositional phrases ("out of", "into", "onto") works *for* us because
it is part of a climactic triplet series, one echoed by the sequence of adjectives ("heavier than air," "fallible," "vain") which
closes the sentence. And how resonant and romantic those
place names become, strung out in a row like that, lingered
over lovingly with the voice.

Prose pleasure need not be restricted to novels. Why not
expect it in Environmental Impact Statements as well? Voice
matters as well as shape, indeed comes from it. To voice we
now turn.

CHAPTER 3

VOICE

The elements of prose style—grammar, syntax, shape, rhythm, emphasis, level, usage—all work as dependent variables. Change one and you change the rest. Rhythm and sound seem, for most prose writers, the most dependent of all: they affect nothing and everything affects them. They do affect something, though. They affect *us*. Rhythm constitutes the most vital of prose's vital life-signs. Rhythmless, unemphatic prose always indicates that something has gone wrong.

TIN EARS

Tin ears, insensitivity to the sound of words, indicate that the hearing that registers rhythm has been turned off. Tin ears have become so common that often you can't tell mistakes from mindlessness. Was this sentence written tongue in cheek or only wax in ears?

> Conflict, chaos, competition and combat combine to constitute both the labor and fertilizer of war and the fruit of this is honor.

Too resolute an alliteration, too many "c" sounds:

> Conflict, chaos, competition and combat combine to constitute
> both the labor and fertilizer of war and the fruit of this is honor.

"Fertilizer" and "fruit" doesn't help, either. "Conflict" is a near
synonym for "combat" and overlaps with "competition"; and
if you use "constitute" you don't need "combine." Nor does
"this" refer to anything specific. Yet the sentence conceals a
rhythm waiting for liberation. A little subtle subtraction leads
to this:

> Combat, competition, and chaos constitute the fertilizer of war and
> the fruit of this fertilizer is honor.

One further change—"constitute the fertilizer of" = "fertil-
ize"—yields a sentence with a sound and shape of its own:

> Combat, competition, and chaos fertilize war and produce its
> fruit—honor. (LF 50%)

We've kept the alliterative yoking of the opening triplet phrase
and created a rhythmically emphatic place of honor for—
honor.

The Official Style, deaf and blind, manages to create
rhythm and shape only by accident. So, for example, a U.S.
government attorney refuses to talk about a controversial spy
case with commendable, if desperate, pertinacity:

> I can't comment. We will not comment. We are not going to
> comment.

This three-segment climax has been used since classical times
(when it was called *tricolon crescens*, each of the three elements
being slightly longer than the previous one, thus building
to a climax) as part of a sentence strategy for building long
rhythmic periodic sentences. Winston Churchill was especially
fond of it:

Victory at all costs, victory in spite of all terror, victory however long and hard the road may be...

This is not the end. It is not even the beginning of the end. But it is, perhaps, the end of the beginning.

The Official Style creates tin ears, and when the ear atrophies, any hope of colloquial emphasis or climax goes down the drain. But when there is a voice to begin with, things are much easier to fix. Look at this flawed diamond:

There is not a sign of life in the whole damned paper (with the possible exception of line 72).

A cinch to fix. Reverse the order.

With the possible exception of line 72, there is not a sign of life in the whole damn paper.

Terrific!

CHANGE-UPS

Sometimes you can notice a colloquial voice change abruptly to an Official Style one: "This point just emphasizes the need of repeated experience for properly utilizing the various sense modalities." The sentence breaks in half after "experience." We expect a finish like, "to use all the senses," and get instead an Official Style translation. Here is a scholar doing the same thing, this time from sentence to sentence:

Official Style

The establishment of an error detection mechanism is necessary to establish a sense of independence in our own movement planning and correction.

Change-up to Plain English

Unless we know we are doing something wrong, we can't correct it.

Change-ups like this emphasize the voicelessness of the Official Style.

Voice usually gets squeezed out of student prose by the Official Style. So we should celebrate an exception, a geography paper with real ears:

> Twice daily, at sunrise and sunset, a noisy, smokeridden train charges into the stillness of the Arabian desert. Winding about the everchanging windblown sand dunes, the "Denver Zephyr" not only defies the fatal forces of the notorious deserts, but for the nonnative, offers an extraordinary encounter with the tightly closed Saudi society.

The "s" assonance—sunrise, sunset, noisy, smokeridden, stillness—works, and so does "fatal forces"; and "forces" echoes part of "notorious," which, with "deserts," defines those forces. The sentence allows the voice a full tonal range, a chance for pitch to rise and fall, and a chance to build a climax on "tightly closed Saudi society" as well. This expanded tonal range, alas, went unappreciated by the instructor: the paper was marked down for being too "journalistic." No good deed goes unpunished.

I'm suggesting that writers should become self-conscious about the sound of words. Once our ears have had their consciousness raised, they'll catch the easy problems as they flow from the pen—"however clever" will become "however shrewd" in the first draft—and the harder ones will seem easier to revise.

ARRHYTHMIA ATTACKS

Now for some arrhythmia attacks from a recent batch of undergraduate papers. The first illustrates the power of a single verb—or lack of one.

> Reputation is also a serious consideration for native Trojans.

Why not:

> Trojans worship Reputation. (LF 66%)

The wordiness of the following sentence lends it an unintended faintly lubricious air:

> The first duty of female characters in the drama of this period is to illustrate the various dimensions of the male protagonist.

Why not:

> In drama of this period female characters must above all illuminate the male protagonist. (LF 36%)

And how about

> Both film and song ask the eternal questions of young adulthood.

as a revision of

> A good measure of this appeal can be traced to the fact that both the visual medium of the film and aural medium of the song confront the young person with eternal questions of young adulthood. (LF 69%)

The revision, by keeping the sentence short, preserves the natural ending emphasis for "young adulthood," and so gives the voice someplace to go. Try reading both aloud several times. See what I mean?

It is not only student prose which has lost its voice but business writing as well. Here a businessman tells us about his firm's new health plan:

> When the sorting of the various problems was taking place, additional vitamins were introduced, cocktails reduced to a minimum, and a regular exercise program begun.

A natural *tricolon crescens* springs forth:

> While the plan was being started up, we took vitamins, cut down on the booze, and began a regular exercise program.

Consider now two longer examples of contrasting prose voices. The first comes from a bureaucrat at the Michigan Department of Environmental Quality. In the second, the target of the bureaucrat's threat replies to it. First the threat.

> It has come to the attention of the Department of Environmental Quality that there has been recent unauthorized activity on the above referenced parcel of property. You have been certified as the legal landowner and/or contractor who did the following unauthorized activity: Construction and maintenance of two wood debris dams across the outlet stream of Spring Pond. A permit must be issued prior to the start of this type of activity....The Department has been informed that one or both of the dams partially failed during a recent rain event, causing debris dams and flooding at downstream locations. We find that dams of this nature are inherently hazardous and cannot be permitted....Failure to comply with this request, or any further unauthorized activity on the site, may result in this case being referred for elevated enforcement action....

60

The authentic Official Style: land becomes a "parcel of property," "rain" becomes a "rain event," and the threat of a fine turns into "elevated enforcement action." Passives, prepositional-phrase trains, a full deployment. But note the *voice*—the genuine niggling mindlessness of a bureaucrat on autopilot.

The perpetrator of this "unauthorized activity on the site" replied:

> A couple of beavers are in the (state unauthorized) process of con-structing and maintaining two wood "debris" dams across the outlet stream of my Spring Pond. While I did not pay for, nor autho-rize, their dam project, I think they would be highly offended that you call their skillful use of natural building materials "debris."...As to your dam request [that] the beavers first must fill out a dam permit prior to the start of this type of dam activity, my first dam question to you is: are you trying to discriminate against my Spring Pond Beavers or do you require all dam beavers throughout this State to conform to said dam request? If you are not discriminating against these particular beavers, please send me completed copies of all those other applicable beaver dam permits....I seriously hope you are not selectively enforcing this dam policy—or once again both I and the Spring Pond Beavers will scream prejudice! (*Wall Street Journal*, 3/30/98; the article concludes: "The Michigan De-partment of Environmental Quality informs us that the case has been closed.")

The voice of common sense, but sensible enough to clothe itself in the insane logic of the bureaucracy.

THE PARAMEDIC METHOD, FULL FORM

Often, when dealing with the Official Style, we must try revis-ing a passage even if we are not sure what it means. In these cases, we may begin to understand the special terms by trying to fathom their relationship. Practice such a "naive analysis," a "revise-to-understand exercise," on the following wonderfully arrhythmic sentence from a book about rhythm!

> Rhythm is that property of a sequence of events in time which produces in the mind of the observer the impression of proportion between the directions of the several events or groups of events of which the sequence is composed.

Look at what the prepositional-phrase strings do to the rhythm of this definition of rhythm:

> Rhythm is that property
> > *of* a sequence
> > *of* events
> > *in* time
> > > which produces
> > *in* the mind
> > *of* the observer the impression
> > *of* proportion
> > *between* the directions
> > *of* the several events or groups
> > *of* events
> > *of* which the sequence is composed.

Can you revise in a way to show that the writer has mastered his subject as well as written about it? Can you use the revision to clarify what the writer has obscured, drag his meaning from the depths of his prose? Try it, using the full form of the Paramedic Method to help:

1. Circle the prepositions.
2. Circle the "is" forms.
3. Ask, "Who's kicking who?" "Where's the action?"
4. Put this action in a simple (not compound) active verb.
5. Start fast—no slow windups.
6. Write out each sentence on a blank sheet of paper and mark off its basic rhythmic units with a "/".
7. Mark off sentence lengths in the passage with a "/".
8. Read the passage aloud with emphasis and feeling.

Sentence length is one of the easiest PM tests to apply. Take a piece of your prose and a red pencil and draw a slash after every sentence. Two or three pages ought to make a large enough sample. If the red marks occur at regular intervals, you have, as they used to say in the Nixon White House, a problem. You can chart the problem another way, if you like. Choose a standard length for one sentence and then do a bar graph. If it looks like this,

dandy. If like this,

not so dandy. Obviously, no absolute quantitative standards exist for how much variety is good, how little bad, but the principle couldn't be easier: vary your sentence lengths. Naturally enough, complex patterns will fall into long sentences and emphatic conclusions work well when short. But no rules prevail except Avoid Monotony.

The following passage certainly obeys this inviolable rule. It comes from a brilliantly written World War II memoir by Brendan Phibbs, *The Other Side of Time*. Dr. Phibbs has been talking about the self-dramatizing, self-serving American General George Patton, and moves from there to Patton's mirror opposite, General Lucien Truscott:

> And now, we said more happily, consider…Truscott.…Men like this are stamped, early in life, and the outlines of the mold spell honesty. They fill the mold without effort; it fits them and they have no question about who they are and what they can do. They're free of the need to grimace and prance; they're free to spend themselves on a cause, for an ideal, scorning advantage and chaining the ego in some remote corner to babble and shriek and rattle its shackles. Having won, they're satisfied with the achievement; they're not driven to seek their value in the gaze and the wonder of others, and they walk off into the quiet corners of history where the truth lives, grinning to watch impostors scribbling their worthless names across the walls of the public baths.

The quiet corners of history where the truth lives—what a wonderful phrase. What creates the rhythm? The sense of authentic voice? Of sentences with a shape which energizes meaning? Well, we might start with Rule 7 of the PM, sentence length. Let's graph them. Graphing is much easier when you write on an electronic screen; simple and cheap graphing programs lie ready to hand.

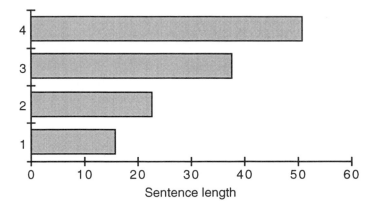

A varied, climactic sentence length. But that only begins to describe how it works. Let's apply Rule 6, and mark off basic rhythmic units.

> And now, we said more happily, consider...Truscott....Men like this are stamped, / early in life, / and the outlines of the mold spell / honesty. / They fill the mold without effort; / it fits them / and they have no question about who they are / and what they can do. / They're free of the need to grimace and prance; / they're free to spend themselves on a cause, / for an ideal, / scorning advantage / and chaining the ego / in some remote corner / to babble and shriek and rattle its shackles. / Having won, / they're satisfied with the achievement; / they're not driven to seek their value in the gaze and the wonder of others, / and they walk off into the quiet corners of history where the truth lives, / grinning to watch impostors scribbling their worthless names / across the walls of the public baths.

What do the rhythmic units look like when diagramed?

> Men like this are stamped, /
> early in life, /
> and the outlines of the mold spell /
> honesty. /
> They fill the mold without effort; /
> it fits them /
> and they have no question about who they are /
> and what they can do. /
> They're free of the need to grimace and prance; /
> they're free to spend themselves on a cause, /
> for an ideal, /
> scorning advantage /
> and chaining the ego /
> in some remote corner /
> to babble and shriek and rattle its shackles. /
> Having won, /
> they're satisfied with the achievement; /

they're not driven to seek their value in the gaze and the wonder
of others, /
and they walk off into the quiet corners of history where the truth
lives, /
grinning to watch impostors scribbling their worthless names /
across the walls of the public baths.

I don't claim this division is linguistically correct, whatever that
might mean. Just the opposite. It is a quick and easy method
any of us can use to chart our own reading of a passage, to
imagine how our voice might embody the prose rhythm. Diagraming makes us specify, *become self-conscious about*, our own
rhythmic interpretation. There's no better way to spot how
sentence rhythm and shape works than to use Rules 6–8 of
the PM. Again:

6. Write out each sentence on a blank sheet of paper and
   mark off its basic rhythmic units with a "/".
7. Mark off sentence length with a "/".
8. Read the passage aloud with emphasis and feeling.

What have they told us here? Well, that the basic rhythmic units, at least as I hear them, vary markedly in length.
Second, that the passage invites stress on a series of crucial
words. Again, let me show you what I mean:

Men like this are stamped, /
early in life, /
and the outlines of the mold spell /
honesty. /
They fill the mold without effort; /
it fits them /
and they have no question about who they are /
and what they can do. /
They're free of the need to grimace and prance; /
they're free to spend themselves on a cause, /
for an ideal, /

scorning advantage /
and chaining the ego /
in some remote corner /
to babble and shriek and rattle its shackles. /
Having won, /
they're satisfied with the achievement; /
they're not driven to seek their value in the gaze and the wonder
of others, /
and they walk off into **the quiet corners of history where the truth
lives**, /
grinning to watch impostors scribbling their worthless names /
across the walls of the public baths.

The PM lends itself naturally to the typographic express-
ivity of an electronic screen. The two work together to give
anyone who cares about prose the power to analyze how a
passage works. The simple typographical diagram I've just
invented immediately tells us more about the passage. It builds
toward a definite climax in a memorable phrase, sets up a
strong emphasis on **honesty** and develops from that a medi-
tation that ends up being about **the quiet corners of history
where the truth lives**. And did you notice how many strong
verb forms, how many actions, the passage contains?

stamped
spell honesty
fill the mold
what they can *do*
grimace and *prance*
spend themselves on a cause
chaining the ego
babble and *shriek* and *rattle* its shackles
Having *won*
driven to seen
walk off into the quiet corners
grinning to *watch* impostors
scribbling their worthless names

The passage recreates for us how history is both acted and reenacted, how it happens and how we seek its truth, waiting there for us in quiet corners. Phibbs wants to describe how we respond to social situations, how we elicit *from* them what we bring *to* them.

Now, by way of contrast, here is a passage of genuinely awesome arrhythmic unintelligibility from an American sociologist. It talks about, as the editor explains—in as much as it has been given me to understand him, much less the sociologist—the background expectancies of situations which make social interaction possible. That is to say, it covers— I think—much the same ground as the Phibbs passage.

> The properties of indexical expressions and indexical actions are ordered properties. These consist of organizationally demonstrable sense, or facticity, or methodic use, or agreement among "cultural colleagues." Their ordered properties consist of organizationally demonstrable rational properties of indexical expressions and indexical actions. Those ordered properties are ongoing achievements of the concerted commonplace activities of the investigators. The demonstrable rationality of indexical expressions and indexical actions retains over the course of its managed production by members the character of ordinary, familiar, routinized, practical circumstances.

Does it *have* to be this way? Or is Official Style prose itself a form of professional grimacing and prancing ? Using the PM as your guide, contrast the two passages. They make a revealing pair.

I've not found a satisfactory way to indicate prose rhythm in a printed book. But try reading aloud these two passages we've examined, one after the other. Don't hurry. And don't read them in a monotone. Let the pitch and timbre of your voice vary. Try out various combinations of pitch, stress, and timing. (There are several ways to read the Phibbs passage, for example.) You can mark pitch variation with a wavy up-and-down line above the text, for a start. And mark musical rests (#, ##, ###) after each phrase and sentence. Try reading each passage aloud, having someone else time you and observe where you pause and for how long. The first passage projects a recognizable voice; it is literally "readable." The second passage, academic prose at its most voiceless, is obviously meant to be read—skimmed—silently.

A VOICE FROM THE '60S

Prose varies widely in the performance instructions that it gives. Official Style academic prose gives very few. The voice has nowhere to go, no natural place to rise and fall, hurry and pause. Metronome prose: tick-tock, tick-tock, tick-tock. For extreme contrast, consider now a prose trip down nostalgia lane which offers lots of performance instructions. A sociology professor has taped a hippie guru telling us what it was like up at Big Sur in the sixties. Try marking the performance instructions; underline, double underline, use quotation marks, whatever.

> When I first got up there, it was a real romantic kind of picture. Man, it was kind of foggy. There were those really beautiful people—men, women, kids, dogs and cats, and campfires. It seemed quiet and stable. And I really felt like love was about me. I thought, "This is the place, man. It was happening. I don't have to do it. I would just kind of fit in and do my thing and that would be like a groove."
>
> After we were there about fifteen or twenty minutes, I heard the people bitching and moaning. I listened to it for awhile and circulated around to hear more about it, and, man, I couldn't believe it. Here they were secure in their land—beautiful land, where they could be free—and all these people were doing was bitching and moaning. I thought, "Oh, shit, man! Do I have to go into this kind of shit again where I gotta step in and get heavy and get ratty and get people to start talking? Do I have to get them to be open and get in some dialogue and get some communication going and

organization? What the —— is wrong with the leadership here, that this kind of state of affairs is happening? And why do I have to do it again? Man, I'm through with it. I just got through with hepatitis and double pneumonia and...—— it!" Then I really felt bad. (Lewis Yablonsky, *The Hippie Trip* [New York: Pegasus, 1968], p. 91)

This is speech, for a start. Hippie speech, heavily syncopated speech, sliding quickly over interim syllables from heavy stress to heavy stress: "first," "romantic," "foggy," "really," "love." Once you know the syncopated pattern, it is easy to mark up a passage like this. But if you don't know the pattern? Imagine yourself a foreigner trying to read this passage with a natural emphasis. It does sometimes give natural rhythmic clues. "This is the *place*, man. It was *happening*. I don't *have* to do it." The arrangement of the words underscores the sense—the scene has become the actor and the actor the scene. So, too, the alliterative repetition of "go into," "gotta step in," "get heavy," "get ratty," "get people," gives us a clear performance clue. But the passage by itself does not include a full guide to its performance. (You needed to be part of the scene to talk this talk like a native. Hippie speech was an *argot*, a special way of speaking used to dramatize a special way of living. The guru quoted above hadn't always talked this way. I know—he was in my class at Yale before the '60s "came down.")

THE TRADITIONAL WAY TO PERFORM PROSE

How can prose include a performance guide, anyway? Especially complex prose of the sort the Official Style usually embodies? In the past, it has done so by building up patterns of repetition, balance, antithesis, and parallelism. This package of systemic controls, usually called a "periodic sentence," has been the traditional way to control a long, complex sentence since classical Greece. The periodic style has been what we might call the "good" Official Style in Western stylistic

We don't write prose like this anymore, and are not used to reading it. The diagrammatic analysis in figure 7 should help a modern reader *visualize* the structure. It works by adding elements in parallel:

> I look with pleasure on my book,
> and deliver it to the world

The parallel elements often create a contrast:

> some words are *budding,*
> and some *falling away*

Or a repetitive list:

> *sudden fits of inadvertency* will surprize vigilance,
> *slight avocations* will seduce attention,
> and *casual eclipses of the mind* will darken learning

Often the antitheses form the antithetical pattern *chiasmus*, with which we've already become acquainted.

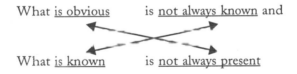

The Official Style often embodies *lists.* The periodic style will hang its list of elements from a single lead word:

> **who** will distinguish
> **who** will consider

Or:

> **that** no dictionary
> **that** a whole life
> **that** even a whole life

history. It has striven for the Official attributes of pu
mality, authoritative impressiveness, solemnity even,
way that *emphasizes* voice rather than etiolating it.
sents true solemnity, a counterstatement to the prose
been revising. It *designs* a long sentence under strict
not a shopping bag stuffed with words.

Any discussion of the Official Style should conside
one instance of its legitimate ancestor, the periodic st
is an example by the great master of the periodic
English, Samuel Johnson. He speaks about his design
piling the first great dictionary of the English langu

> When I am animated by this wish [to honor his count
> with pleasure on my book, however defective, and delive
> world with the spirit of a man that has endeavored we
> will immediately become popular I have not promised
> a few wild blunders, and risible absurdities, from whicl
> of such multiplicity was ever free, may for a time furnish
> laughter, and harden ignorance in contempt; but useful
> will at last prevail, and there never can be wanting som
> tinguish desert; who will consider that no dictionary
> tongue ever can be perfect, since while it is hastening t
> tion, some words are budding, and some falling away; th
> life cannot be spent upon syntax and etymology, and tl
> whole life would not be sufficient; that he, whose desig
> whatever language can express, must often speak of wh
> not understand; that a writer will sometimes be hurried
> ness to the end, and sometimes faint with weariness un
> which *Scaliger* compares to the labours of the anvil, and
> that what is obvious is not always known, and what is
> not always present; that sudden fits of inadvertency wi
> vigilance, slight avocations will seduce attention, and casu
> of the mind will darken learning; and that the writer s
> in vain trace his memory at the moment of need, for t
> yesterday he knew with intuitive readiness, and which
> uncalled into his thoughts tomorrow. (From the prefa
> *English Dictionary*, in *Johnson: Prose and Poetry*, ed. Mor
> [Cambridge: Harvard University Press, 1967], pp. 322-

that he
that a writer
that what is obvious
that sudden fits

These clear and repeated shapes *visualize* meaning in precisely the way we considered in chapter 2. They also give the voice a set of *performing instructions*. In figure 8, simply by using three sizes of type, I indicate the obvious stresses. Notice how the *voice* plays a counterpoint over the *shape*, sometimes reinforcing it and sometimes creating a different pattern? It is the absence of this counterpoint, more often than not, which makes the Official Style so insipidly lifeless.

A PAUSE FOR REFLECTION

Whether you relish periodic prose as I do or not, you ought to try in your own writing to give equally good performance instructions. And, in your long sentences, to maintain equally good syntactic and stylistic control. For, again, that is what sentence length, rhythm, and sound are—a series of instructions, of controls, for how your sentences should be performed. And if your reader takes pleasure in performing your prose, you have her on your side. She is acting in your play.

We've seen how sentences become shapeless when the voice goes out of them. Prose that is not voiced becomes shapeless and unemphatic in the same way that an unexercised muscle loses its tone. And it works the other way, too. If we do not look at a piece of prose, attempt to perform it, we'll cease to hear real voices, our own and others', when we speak. Writing and speaking form a spiral. If they intensify each other, the spiral goes up. If they don't, each drives the other down.

CHAPTER 4

SKOTISON!

A legendary anecdote reports that an American general once asked Winston Churchill to read the draft of a speech. "Too many passives and too many zeds," Churchill commented. Asked to explain his comment, Churchill said:

> Too many Latinate polysyllabics like "systematize, prioritize, finalize." And then the passives. What if I had said—instead of "We shall fight on the beaches"—"Hostilities will be engaged with our adversary on the coastal perimeter"?

In the previous three chapters, we have been practicing a revision method that moves from the general's Official Style eleven words to Churchill's plain English six. "We shall fight on the beaches" rallied England to its Finest Hour. The Official Style's "Hostilities will be engaged with our adversary on the coastal perimeter" would have elicited first a "Huh?" and then probably a "Not by me they won't." It cries out for *inaction*. By now, we've seen all the Official Style attributes which create this inclination for inaction:

> It hides *actor* and *action* in passive and impersonal constructions. Never "I decided" but always "It was decided that...."

It displaces the action from simple verb into a complex construction. "I see" becomes "A visionary ability can be obtained which permits...."

It uses a Latinate diction—all those "zed" verbs like "prioritize" and all those "shun" nouns like "prioritization."

It adores the slow sentence start, the long windup while the writer thinks up something to say: "One can easily see that in confronting a situation of this sort...."

It follows faithfully a formula of prepositional phrases + "is" + more prepositional phrases. "The fact of the matter in a case of this sort is that...."

These strings of prepositional phrases make it *shapeless*. The eye can offer no help to the sense.

Because it offers the voice no chance to emphasize or harmonize, you cannot read it out loud. It is unspeakable.

It takes twice as long as its plain English translation. In the fullness of its best, it embodies the attitudes, and complacent habits of inaction, of a large, impersonal, arbitrary bureaucracy.

Finally, the Official Style is *euphemistic*. Everyone sees this now, and laughs at it. Buzzword indexes abound. Rats become "small faunal species," smells dress up as "olfactory impacts." Or, in the new "politically correct" versions, "short" = "vertically challenged," "fat" = "possessing an alternative body image," "dumb" = "negatively gifted." Correct grammar becomes "ethnocentric white patriarchal restructuring of language." Every misbehaving child has "oppositional defiance disorder." The Official Style, in whatever new dress, always dresses up in a special terminology.

WHY DOES THE OFFICIAL STYLE THRIVE?

During the two decades since the first edition of *Revising Prose* appeared, the forces generating the Official Style have

all grown stronger. Government, in spite of many "privatiz-
ings," just keeps growing. Professional specialization grips our
lives with an ever stronger hand, and professional languages
grow ever more arcane and incomprehensible. Business
organizations merge into ever larger, and therefore more
bureaucratic, conglomerations. Even the language of business—where, you would think, a plain style would be most
prized—has grown Official. As a recent book on management
gurus put it: "There seems to be something in the water in
business schools or at management conferences that destroys
people's capacity to speak plainly or write clearly" (John
Micklethwait and Adrian Wooldridge, *The Witch Doctors*
[Times Books, 1996], p. 12). Just when time has become our
most precious commodity, we are like to drown in long-
windedness.

Some years ago, the American literary critic Lionel Trill-
ing wrote: "A spectre haunts our culture. It is that people will
eventually be unable to say 'We fell in love and married'...but
will, as a matter of course, say, 'Their libidinal impulses being
reciprocal, they integrated their individual erotic drives and
brought them within the same frame of reference.'" So, now,
the preacher begins his sermon with "Had Moses not inter-
faced with Pharaoh...." So now the lawyer resigns as chief of
staff of Congress's Joint Tax Committee not because *it pays
badly* but because "while this job is clearly the best job in
America for a tax lawyer, *one of the unfortunate downsides is
that it causes one to be fiscally challenged.*" So now the director
of marketing for General Motors: "We still don't know how
good the new vehicles are because we have been so availability-
constrained." What he meant was, "We don't know how well
the new cars will sell because we haven't made enough to find
out."

Why, you might ask, does this long-winded style continue
to thrive? The sums you need to reckon up the savings are
pretty simple: half the paper cost, half the keyboarding costs,
half the time to read, a third the time to understand—anybody can do these sums. And anybody can learn to revise the

Official Style into a plain dynamic one. It takes some effort, as the previous chapters teach; indeed it does. But it saves even more effort, effort and time. Why, then, do we put up with the Official Style? Why do we seem, even, to cultivate this ugly, melting waste of time? Why are academic writers so fond of it? Or, to put the question another way, what trouble may you be getting into if you revise it into plain English? A book devoted to such revision has to pose this question, at least. Give fair warning to its readers. Here's my best shot at some answers.

Ego leads the pack. The Official Style is, or is commonly thought to be, more imposing. It speaks with organizational authority. Like a football helmet and shoulder pads, it makes the writer look taller, wider, more intimidating.

Fear contends with Ego for the starring role. If you work in a large organization, standing out from the crowd can kill you. Don't get identified with *any* action, because if it goes wrong, you'll get the blame. Imitate the style you encounter all around you. "Diversity" has no place in the world of prose style.

Litigation comes not far behind. In so pervasively litigious a society as our own, incomprehensible prose has come into its own as a protection against being sued. People are less likely to sue you if they can't understand what you have said. And you can put up a better defense if you can argue that you haven't said it anyway. The Official Style serves both purposes equally well.

Oddly enough, print itself must take some of the blame. It permits no direct voice. Its presentational conventions—black-and-white, continuous lineation, uniform typeface—allow only indirect emphasis. Acres of Official Style print have spawned a new kind of reading—Speed Reading—which encourages reading only for a key island of significance in a sea of ritualistic verbosity. Ever since McLuhan called print a "visual" medium, we've thought of it that way, but at its most profound level it doesn't work on the visual cortex at all. Print aims to be invisible, *unnoticed* by the eye, so that we can

---

concentrate on the thought. A mode of presentation like electronic text, which invokes eye and ear, makes the Official Style hard to bear.

Professional mystification plays a strong role. We might call this the ego of an intellectual class. The Official Style comes in a variety of dialects, but they are all professional languages. The language of the law came first, as old as written history, with the Greek and Latin patois of medical terminology a close second. Governmental bureaucracies have always cherished a special language to make them more priestly and witch-doctorish, and hence more authoritative. They spoke the language of a deep mystery. When the current academic and professional specializations came to the fore a century ago, they each adopted a dialect of the Official Style to prove that they were scientific. The less scientific they were, the more Official their Style.

Self-mystification plays more than a bit part. If a bureaucracy uses the Official Style for very long, it begins to fool *itself*. After this happens—and it has happened in every government bureau and academic discipline—plain English looks like *satire*. If you do a *Revising Prose* number on an Official Style report, you are pointing out that the emperor has no clothes on. You are writing satire, and satire is a dangerous business. *Revising Prose* reader, be warned!

SKOTISON! DARKEN IT!

The great Roman rhetorician Quintilian tells of a rhetoric teacher who taught his pupils to make everything they said intentionally obscure. *Skotison*, he would tell them in Greek: *Darken it!* Successful obscurity elicited this praise from the teacher: "So much the better: even I could not understand it!" A later Latin writer, Ausonius, confessed to a similar relish for obscurity: "I might tell thee outright; but for more pleasure I will talk in mazes and with speech drawn out get full enjoyment." And, in the eighteenth century, Samuel Johnson talked of the same delight in intentional obscurity: "There is a mode of style for which I know not that the masters of oratory have yet found a name, a style by which the most evident truths are so obscured that they can no longer be perceived, and the most familiar propositions so disguised that they cannot be known. Every other kind of eloquence is the dress of sense, but this is the mask..." (*Idler*, 36). In my *Handlist of Rhetorical Terms* (University of California Press, second edition 1991), I call this love of obscurity, this cultivation of darkness, *skotison*.

The "something in the water" at business schools is *skotison*. Today we meet it everywhere we look. It mixes together the shoulder-padded egotism we've discussed above with our delight in fooling others and, even more, in fooling ourselves. The scholarly journal *Literature and Philosophy* sponsors a yearly "bad writing" contest in which readers send it samples of the worst prose they have encountered during the year. Three contest prize-winners follow, all wonderful examples of *skotison*. The first comes from a Marxist social critic, the second from a philosopher, the third from a literary critic. Each is a single sentence.

The Marxist social critic:

> The triumphant moment in which a new systemic dominant gains ascendancy is therefore only the diachronic manifestation of a constant struggle for the perpetuation and reproduction of its dominance, a struggle which must continue throughout its life course, accompanied at all moments by the systemic or structural antagonism of those older and newer modes of production that resist assimilation or seek deliverance from it.

The philosopher:

> Indeed dialectical critical realism may be seen under the aspect of Foucauldian strategic reversal—of the unholy trinity of Parmenidean/

Platonic/Aristotelean provenance; of the Cartesian-Lockean-Humean-Kantian paradigm; of foundationalisms (in practice, fideistic foundationalisms) and irrationalisms (in practice, capricious exercises of the will-to-power or some other ideologically and/or psycho-somatically buried source) new and old alike; of the primordial failing of western philosophy, ontological monovalence, and its close ally, the epistemic fallacy with its ontic dual; of the analytic problematic laid down by Plato, which Hegel served only to replicate in his actualist monovalent analytic reinstatement in transfigurative reconciling dialectical connection, while in his hubristic claims for absolute idealism he inaugurated the Comtean, Kierkegaardian and Nietzschean eclipses of reason, replicating the fundaments of positivism through its transmutation route to the superidealism of a Baudrillard.

The literary critic:

When interpreted from within the ideal space of the myth-symbol school, Americanist masterworks legitimized hegemonic understanding of American history expressively totalized in the metanarrative that had been reconstructed out of (or more accurately read into) these masterworks.

Obscure prose of this sort is by no means uncommon in the modern academic world. In the twenty years since *Revising Prose* first appeared, academic disciplines have grown more Official, not less, and prided themselves on their increasing obscurity. The social sciences, which formerly led the way, have ceded pride of place to the humanities, where the special field called "literary theory" has devised a special language of its own, of which these passages seem to be examples. I won't offer revisions of these passages because, since I cannot understand them, I cannot revise them. In fairness to my own inadequacies in this regard, I should add that other readers, more qualified than I in the disciplines invoked, have been equally mystified.

Surely, mystification—*skotison*—is the main aim here. Defenders of mystifying styles often offer just this argument. Writers who make the reader puzzle out a meaning give that reader better value for money. Digging up the meaning is half the fun. Obscurity ensures rarity. To object that you can't understand such prose misses the point. It belongs to another genre altogether, *the rhetoric of display*. It aims to display the writer's knowledge, his in-group status. He, or she, *knows the secret handshakes!* Knows all the arcane terms, and can display them in a simulacrum of English syntax.

When Official styles develop in a closed professional field, they turn in on themselves, become more interested in display and less in argument. Anyone who writes with an eye toward ordinary understanding is stigmatized as a "popularizer." It has happened before and—given the persistence of ego, fear, fashion, and our human love of euphemism—will happen again. When you grow up in such a style, and nowadays every American student does, plain prose makes you feel undressed. As a student, and as a mature professional too, you want to imitate the accepted writers in your field, and they write in various professional dialects of the Official Style. Naturally, piously, you want to imitate them. You assume that the rhetoric of display substitutes for argument. And often, if you get it right, you are right. Stylistic imitation proves that you've joined the club, and you get a good grade. Or a published article.

How to behave in an Official Style world, whether to persist in trying to make ordinary sense or give in to the *skotison*, I will discuss in chapter 6, "Why Bother?" But we all should be aware that the Official Style, in the highest stages of its development, not only discourages plain sense but abandons it altogether for the pleasures of display. Understanding this development will spare readers who want to make out the plain sense—the readers of this book—much vexation of spirit.

A PAUSE FOR REFLECTION

We ought not, though, close this brief discussion of *skotison* on a churlish, puritanical note. After all, it springs from linguistic play as well as humorless self-importance. We all enjoy the special language we use for our special concerns. The computer industry, which is not usually accused of taking itself too seriously, started out with a special language it had to invent for a new world. It then started using it for ordinary life, so that every meeting became an "interface" and every dullard a "slow chip." The euphemistic jargon of political correctness is used, as often as not, with humor and irony. The Official Business Style that is taught in schools of management spawns a playful jargon. From a recent article in the *Los Angeles Times*, I learn that the CEO of a much-touted startup, when he had to report a huge fourth-quarter loss, changed his title to "Visionary." The former chairman of a coffee company styled himself "Chief Coffee Officer." "Evangelist" and "Vibe Guy" have joined COO, CEO, CBO, and all those square titles on rectangular business cards. And you make a plan by "dimensionalizing," look ahead by "helicoptering," and read between the lines by seeking out "white space opportunities." Sometimes, especially if your ox isn't being gored, it is more fun to sit back, put your feet up, and savor the throughput. *Skotison!*

CHAPTER 5

ELECTRONIC
LITERACY

When you display written words on an electronic screen rather than imprint them on paper, reading itself changes radically; electronic "literacy" turns out to differ in fundamental ways from "print" literacy. And electronic literacy increasingly dominates the workplace. Anyone working in present-day America confronts these radical changes in expressive medium, in "literacy," in reading and writing, every day. Even a practical, hands-on guide like *Revising Prose* must pause to reflect on these changes, for they have transformed how the written word lives and works in human life.

Changes close to home first. We have already noticed how word processors enhance prose revision. They make it much easier not only to get the words "down" (though "on screen" rather than "on paper") but to take them up and move them around. And the speed with which revision takes place means, often, that more revision can take place when writing—as we usually do—under a deadline. No need to go through those one-day retyping turnarounds for each revision. And electronic spelling and grammar checkers and the electronic thesaurus, by speeding up ordinary procedures, further encourage revision. Global searches can find prepositional-phrase strings and tell you if every main verb is *is*. Use global search-and-replace to put a space and return at the end of each sentence for a page or two and you'll get a pretty good idea of sentence-length variation. Word-counters and calculators make computing the Lard Factor much faster. And changes in layout and typography become a handy analytical tool to find one's way in the Official Style's pathless prose woods. Because the computer is a rule-based device, it lends itself to a rule-based revision method. All in all, prose paramedics have never had it so easy.

VISUALIZATION AND VOICING

But digital text has changed literacy more profoundly than these helpful easements suggest. Most important, the relationship between verbal and visual communication is changing. More and more, images both supplement and replace written information. For statistical presentation of all sorts, old-fashioned pie charts and bar graphs have given way to more imaginative and three-dimensional renderings. Even simple spreadsheet programs encourage the visualization of numeric data. And computer graphics now routinely model all kinds of complex dynamic processes in three dimensions and real time.

We are so used to the convention of print—linear, regular left-to-right and top-to-bottom, black-and-white, uniform font and type size—that we have forgotten how constraining it is. Black-and-white print is remarkable for its power to express conceptual thought but equally so for all the powers it renounces in doing so. No pictures, no color, no perspective. Up to now these things have been just too expensive. No longer. On the electronic screen, you can do them all and a lot more. And as electronic memory gets ever cheaper, they have come within the reach of everyday wordsmiths as well as graphic designers.

The constraints of conventionally printed prose are slowly dissolving. If we can use color, font size and shape, three-dimensional effects such as drop-shadow and the like, then we will use them. If we can intersperse text and graphics with ease, we'll come to depend on the combination. All these changes, in their turn, are changing how we write and indeed how we think. It is no exaggeration to say that electronic textual information has now become three-dimensional. The black-and-white, letters-only convention concentrates on abstract thought—the "meaning"—to the exclusion of everything else. Tonal colorations there will always be—they are what we usually call "style"—but in print they work always beneath the surface, implicit rather than explicit. Bringing them to the surface takes time and trouble. With the electronic word, however, these tonal colorations can be explicit rather than implicit. We are able, literally, to "color" our communications with one another.

And there is no going back, no abjuration of this new realm of communication. If you can write "in color," and choose not to, that too will be a "communication," and usually one you will not want to make. How often nowadays do you watch black-and-white TV? And what does it seem like when you do?

What do these changes imply for literacy in the workplace and the schools and colleges which prepare students for it? Well, for a start, they dramatize a need I have been advocating all through this book, a need to use the visual imagination in reading, writing, and revising. More than ever, we must notice the shape of prose. Up to now, "graphics" people tended to work in one office and "word" people in another. No more. From now on, graphics will be part of a writer's basic training. Words and images are now inextricably intertwined in our common expressive repertoire.

The desktop-publishing revolution reinforces this change at every point. Typography and layout, a special field before, in electronic display become an expressive parameter for all writers. Type fonts have become *allegorical.* They invoke a particular mood, represent an attitude, speak as pictures as well as symbols. The classic creed of the typographer has always been that the written surface should be transparent—never noticed for itself, serving only the meaning shining through its lucid waters. That theory needs adjustment. We will be looking *at* the prose surface as much as looking *through* it. And that is what *Revising Prose* has always had in mind. Revision means exactly this oscillation between looking *at* and looking *through* a prose surface. The natural logic of electronic text leads more naturally to this *at/through* oscillation than does print, and so invites revision in a way fixed print does not.

I've also been arguing that prose—now uniformly read in silence—should be *voiced*, at least in the auditory imagination. The digitized word reinforces and empowers this recommendation as well. Since the last edition of this book, voice communication has become a reality in computer communication. We can now talk to the computer and it can talk back. Soon voicing will be a routine dimension of the electronic word. We will move from voice to writing to image and back again in ways new to humankind. The Official Style pushes prose to its voiceless extreme. We have seen that over and over; *read it aloud* and the Official Style sounds silly, absurdly pompous, often simply pointless. Voice is now returning to writing in ways so structural as to recall an oral culture rather than a written one. *Voiceless* prose won't work much longer.

MULTIMEDIA PROSE

All these changes have come together in an emergent job category—the information designer, a person who suits the information to the expressive medium. At the core of the computer revolution stands a polyvalent code which can be expressed in words, images, or sound. The different parts of the human sensorium now share a common digital code. Obviously, we will not usually want to express the information on a hospital chart in musical form (although it has been done). But information itself is now *designed*. The information designer orchestrates modes of expression. Writing prose has become part of a larger endeavor which must decide first *how the information will be expressed*, through word, image, sound, or a mixture of the three. Plato dreamed of such a union, hoping to find the common focus for all knowledge in mathematics. In more than a manner of speaking, that dream has come true.

Electronic literacy, then, differs markedly from print literacy. It knows how to mix alphabetic information with information coming from image and sound. People at every level communicate in a richer but more complex informational sensorium. Writing has come to mean something different, and writers who don't know, and feel, this find themselves the clerks of a forgotten mood.

Prose style, in the world of the conventional printed book, works in a carefully protected vacuum. Extraneous signals are carefully filtered out. Typography and layout aim to help us concentrate on textual meaning without distracting our attention to themselves. Writers are people who are good with words. Pictures and sounds only distract them. This isolation has encouraged and reinforced the Official Style. It could be unreadable because nobody ever listened to it read aloud. It could be shapeless because nobody ever looked at its shape. Multimedia prose encourages us to look and listen.

VOLATILE TEXT AND TEXTUAL AUTHORITY

Other constitutional changes come with the electronic word. Perhaps foremost, *authority* diffuses itself between writer and reader. Although we seldom think of it in this way, the print medium is fundamentally authoritarian. "In print" means unchangeable. You can't quarrel with it. This penumbra of authority goes back a long way. The Renaissance humanists resurrected the authority of classical Greek and Latin culture by editing that culture's documents into fixed printed texts. The authoritative edition means the unchanging edition, text fixed forever, a lodestone of cultural authority. We still feel that way about print. It *fixes* things.

Electronic text *unfixes* them. It is by nature changeable, anti-authoritarian. If we don't like what it says, we can change it, ornament it, revise it, erase it, mock it in letters indistinguishable from the original ones. Patterns of authority have shifted, become democratized. This democratization means that the electronic word will mean something quite different from the printed one. Anyone interested in writing of any sort must understand this change.

It operates, for a start, upon the role the writer adopts as a writer. When we write we inevitably adopt a social role of some sort. Trying to bring this presentation of self to self-consciousness has been one of our main tasks in this book. Surely all of us have noticed that the self we adopt in computer communication, especially on-line, differs from our "print" self. For reasons I leave to the psychologists, computers have from their beginnings evoked the game and play ranges of human motivation far more strongly than print. The "hacker" personality that created the computer was suffused with the competitive game impulse, but equally with the "for-its-own-sake" impulse to do something just to see if it could be done. This hacker mentality inevitably creeps in whenever we put our fingers on the computer's home row: we hold language more lightly in our hands; our sense of humor stirs; we can't take things, or ourselves, so seriously.

A good predisposition this turns out to be—returning from theory to home concerns—for avoiding the Official Style and its systematic pomposity. The "dignity of print" has a lot to answer for. Let's hope that the electronic word preserves the muse of comedy that has hovered around its creation. At all events, it is something to be alert to if you are writing and revising prose in an electronic world. It has created a new communications decorum.

ALLEGORICAL ALPHABETS

This book is not the place to illustrate the changes in store for us. In the first place, no book can: the book is just what electronic text is transcending. In the second place, *Revising Prose* is a hands-on guide, not a theoretical discussion. But perhaps an example or two can sketch the revolution in typography which the personal computer is bringing about.

The printed book, as we have known it since Gutenberg, depends on print as essentially transparent and unselfconscious—we do not notice it as print. The book may be well designed or ill, and we may register that. But the type selected, the size and shape of the letters, the white space between and around them, does not form part of the meaning. Making all these selections, "specing type" as designers and editors call it, is a production task, not an authorial affair.

All this is now changing. Typography can now be—and I think increasingly will become—allegorical, part of the meaning, an authorial not a production function. This will allow us to *see* prose characteristics that formerly we could only talk about. We will be able to analyze and revise prose in new ways, using new mixtures of alphabet and icon. We can grasp how this process might work by using the font and graphics capabilities available on any graphics monitor.

Here is a typical academic sentence:

> The integration of a set of common value patterns with the internalized need-disposition structure of the constituent personalities is the core phenomenon of the dynamics of social systems.

Huh? The usual shapeless shopping bag of general concepts held together by "is" and prepositional glue. Let's consider three diagrams of its structure, diagrams anyone can construct on a personal computer.

The integration
of a set
of common value patterns
with the internalized need-disposition structure
of the constituent personalities
is the core phenomenon
of the dynamics
of social systems.

The	integration	of a set
of	common value patterns	
with the	internalized need-disposition structure	
of the	constituent personalities	
is the	core phenomenon	
of the	dynamics	
of	social systems.	

The		integration of a set
of	common value	patterns
with the	internalized need-disposition	structure
of the	constituent	personalities
is the	core	phenomenon
of the		dynamics
of	social	systems.

In the first, I have done one of our usual vertical preposition charts, but with a little enhancement to render the pattern more graphic.

The second diagram tries to plot what relationship the general terms bear to one another by listing them separately from the prepositions that glue them together in a string. The separate listing shows you immediately what is wrong: the concepts in the list bear no discernible relationship to one another. Nothing in the concepts themselves tells us how they might be related; the pressures for connection fall entirely on the prepositions. They cannot bear it. Their breakdown is what makes the passage so hard to read. And the qualification of the key terms by adjectives, which themselves represent key terms—"common value patterns," "internalized need-disposition structure," "constituent personalities"—makes things still worse.

So I rearranged the sentence into the third diagram, trying to set off the key words and indicate graphically the three basic levels that compose the sentence. The lack of any genuine relationship, causal or otherwise, between the central words in the right-hand column shows up even more. You can, given the syntax of the sentence, rearrange the central terms several different ways and still make sense of a sort. Try it.

Diagrams like this provide a powerful analytical tool. You needn't sit there cudgeling your brains in paralytic silence. You can start trying to make sense of things right on the screen, using your eyes and hands to help you think. The need to "spec type" stimulates you to explore how the sentence fits together. And you can, by type selection, both display your analysis and demonstrate your attitude toward it.

Now a simpler sentence altogether: "These ideas create a frame for the paragraph." A series of typographical manipulations shows the stages of perception that follow from applying Rules 3 and 4 of the PM—finding the action and putting it in a single, simple verb.

These ideas ᴄʀᴇᴀᴛᴇ ᴀ ꜰʀᴀᴍᴇ ꜰᴏʀ **the paragraph.**

These ideas create a ꜰʀᴀᴍᴇ **for the paragraph.**

These ideas ꜰʀᴀᴍᴇ **the paragraph.**

These ideas frame the paragraph.

I used an outline typeface, one that frames each letter, to echo the "framing" action in the sentence. This kind of punning comment is but one of many available when type selection can be an authorial rather than an editorial function.

In the next example, I changed type to show where, in mid-sentence, the reader gets lost. The second type selection tries to depict this confusion visually.

ORDINARY TYPOGRAPHY

However, consciousness does exist and it stimulates an antagonistic relationship between the acceptance of the role of self-consciousness and the disregard of the knowledge which is indigenous to consciousness for the adaptation of a more sentimental role.

ALLEGORICAL TYPOGRAPHY

However, consciousness does exist and it stimulates an antagonistic relationship between the acceptance of the role of self-consciousness and the disregard of the knowledge which is indigenous to consciousness for the adaptation of a more sentimental role.

You can use a similar technique to spotlight a persistent sound-clash pattern, here a hissing "s," "sh," and "t" in the prose of a biologist whose prose remains persistently tone-deaf:

> Since Darwin initially provided the means of testing for the existence of an evolutionary process and for its significance in accounting for the attributes of living organisms, biologists have accepted with increasing decisiveness the hypothesis that all attributes of life are outcomes of that simple process.

In the next example, also written by a professor, I've tried to portray graphically the shapeless, unfocused prose by printing the passage three times, in typefaces that become progressively easier to read. The first makes us look at the shape of the sentence only, since it is so hard to read the typeface. We have to look *at* rather than *through*. The second is easier, the third easier still. It yields, in turn, to our usual graph of the shopping bag sentence; there I've tried to satirize the wallboard monotony by making the prepositions large and, with a glance at the medieval subject of the passage, in a "medieval" type.

It is one of the paradoxes of the history of rhetoric that what was in Antiquity essentially an oral discipline for the pleading of law cases should have become in the Middle Ages in one of its major aspects, a written discipline for the drawing up of quasi-legal documents.

It is one of the paradoxes of the history of rhetoric that what was in Antiquity essentially an oral discipline for the pleading of law cases should have become in the Middle Ages in one of its major aspects, a written discipline for the drawing up of quasi-legal documents.

It is one of the paradoxes of the history of rhetoric that what was in Antiquity essentially an oral discipline for the pleading of law cases should have become in the Middle Ages in one of its major aspects, a written discipline for the drawing up of quasi-legal documents.

It is one
of the paradoxes
of the history
of rhetoric that what was
in antiquity essentially an oral discipline
for the pleading of law cases should have become
in the Middle Ages
in one
of its major aspects, a written discipline
for the drawing up
of quasi-legal documents.

I've asked students repeatedly how they read large stretches of "Official Style" academic prose; the uniform answer has been, "I skip from key term to key term and guess at their connection." I've tried to depict this habit in the next sentence:

The idea of **action language implies** as the correct approach to the emotions **foregoing** the use of **substantives** in making **emotion-statements** and **employing** for this purpose only **verbs and adverbs** or adverbial locutions.

We might call this "highlighter reading"; it can provide a handy guide for revision. It may someday find its way into the printing conventions for wallboard prose like this, as a kind of running internal summary. Probably, though, it would prove too satirical.

In the following typographical rendering, I've tried to depict visually a sentence slowly running out of gas as it passes through its prepositional-phrase string. I've used italics to emphasize how the vital concept in the sentence has been placed in the least emphatic place possible, just before the sentence peters out completely.

Dr. Heartfelt has earned a reputation for excellence for the sharing of the wisdom of the path of *compassionate service* in the natural healing arts.

Diagraming prose rhythm in a printed book never works well; it goes against the grain of the medium. I was trying, in the following diagram, to visualize a sentence whose first half was metronymically monotonous but whose second half fell into a rhythmical, indeed even symmetrical, pattern. I also thought it might show how a change in typeface can sometimes indicate a quotation more forcefully than quotation marks.

While the whole world	even Roosevelt
felt a sense	of relief
at the escape	from war
at the time	of Munich

Churchill stood up in the House of Commons and
disregarding a storm of protest
somberly declared

𝔚e have sustained a total and unmitigated
𝔡efeat.

A final example springs from pure play. I had picked out a sentence from a student paper—"Etching will always be my love"—because it sounded silly to me. Should it be "I will always love etching"? Not much better. I wondered what typographical enhancement might do to it:

Etching will always be my love.

Etching will always be my love.

Etching will always be my love.

Etching will always be my love.

No luck. It gets sillier and sillier. Can you figure out why?

REFLECTING ON THE ELECTRONIC WORD

I've presented these typographical transformations as tools of analysis, but they are tools of creation as well. The creative revolution in prose expression has, since the last edition of this book, taken several giant steps forward.

Text has, for a start, been put into a *three-dimensional* field. Imagine text floating in space, with a reader flying through this space, going ever deeper into the text. Imagine a text with its general arguments at the surface and the supporting detail existing in smaller and smaller scale as you fly through the space. "3D textual space" may sound odd, but we already talk about text *metaphorically* in this way: we say we are "going deeper" into a text, "getting to the bottom" of an argument, or have "skimmed the surface" of a report.

In addition to being put back into space, text has been put back into time. A mode of presentation called "kinetic typography" presents text in real time, word or phrase at a time, swimming forward to our eyes or receding from them. Kinetic typography has become common in TV ads, and it will be put to other uses as the technique grows more familiar and filters down to desktop programs. This textual animation blends typographic design with choreography; the type begins to dance.

I have no idea where this cornucopia of changes will fetch us up, but clearly prose, and prose revision, will never be the same. Revising the electronic word will be easier, more challenging, creative, and much more fun. The kind of typographical manipulation and commentary we've been toying with hints at the coming metamorphosis of the word. With it will come a new understanding of prose style and, indeed, a new definition of prose itself.

I don't want to extend further this argument about the expressive opportunities created by computer display; as I said earlier, *Revising Prose* is not a theoretical book. But as much as I have said must, I think, be said in any book about prose revision. The electronic word has changed the whole matrix of written expression, just as digitization has transformed the marketplace itself. To ignore this state-change at the one level is as perilous as to ignore it at the other.

Let me end these brief but needful reflections with one that emerges from our labors at prose revision. The logic of a society built on information instead of, or in addition to, goods, will lead us to a self-consciousness about words and the signals they broadcast far greater than now customary. The kind of verbal self-consciousness now restricted to writers and literary critics will, by the technological "logic" of an electronic information society, become a core professional skill. That new conception of prose—as wide as language itself, and as bright and sparkling and changeable as the electronic word can make it—offers a new and lively path whose ending none of us can foresee. The Official Style, shapeless, voiceless, confusing and confused, will find itself under pressure when it walks this path. We'll register its ugliness as clearly as its inefficiency. New reasons why we should bother to revise it.

CHAPTER 6

WHY BOTHER?

Revising Prose argues that the Official Style muddles much of America's prose. In as much as this is true, the paramedic analogy holds and the prose can be revised using simple procedures. We have illustrated the Official Style's attributes: dominantly a noun style; a concept style; a style whose sentences have no artful design, no rhythm, or emphasis; an unreadable, voiceless, impersonal style; a style built on euphemisms; a style with a formulaic sentence structure, "is" plus a string of prepositional phrases before and after. And we've learned how to revise it. A set of do-it-yourself techniques, the Paramedic Method, handles the problem nicely— if sometimes laboriously. But at this point you may well be asking, "Why bother?" Why see in a blind world? Why spend extra time making yourself conspicuous? There are two answers, or rather, two kinds of answers.

THE FIRST KIND OF ANSWER

"If you can see what others can't, you'll get ahead." Certainly. But not always. Clear prose does make for a better school or job application, a better legal brief or progress report or memo. And today, ordinary writing skills are more needed—and more valued—than ever. Writing well can open many doors. Where the Official Style is mandated by rule or custom, however, plain prose may sound simpleminded or even flip. It may even get you in trouble.

What to do? Learn both languages, the Plain and the Official Style. As always in the two millennia of rhetoric's history, there are rules that work but no rules about when to apply those rules. I cannot better the answer that the likes of Aristotle, Cicero, and Quintilian have always returned: learn the rules and then, through experience, train your intuition to apply them effectively. *Stylistic* judgment is, last as well as first, always *political* judgment. That ineluctable equation—which there is no dodging—makes stylistic judgment vital enough to warrant books like this one.

As a political decision, writing plainly constitutes a better decision today than even half a dozen years ago. We live, we are told on all sides, in an information economy. The vital commodity is no longer physical stuff but the information needed to extract it from the earth's crust and process it into goods. But the commodity in short supply—what economists usually study—is not information. We lack not information—we're drowning in that—but the time to make sense of it. The vital commodity turns out to be *human attention*. We might better call our present situation an attention economy than an information one.

Now, in an economy of attention, a cardinal transformation takes place. In a goods economy, the essential artifact is physical stuff. That stuff provides the controlling value. *Things* dominate. The language which describes those things has value only as it describes the things. The people who deal with things—dig materials from the earth's crust, process them, make stuff out of them—occupy center stage. The language used to describe those materials and processes plays a secondary role. If you can use mathematical formulas, that is best. If you have to use words, use words that point directly to the things. But the *words* rank second to the *things*. This relationship inverts in an economy of attention. Words *allocate attention*. They mediate between information and the people who use it. Words now occupy center stage, and stuff moves to the wings.

In a goods economy, suppose somebody writes an Official Style sentence that takes too long to tell its tale, and confuses the tale into the bargain. Well, so what? The stuff gets through, and that's the important thing. If you can save time and money *making the stuff*, good for you. That matters. But nobody saves any real money making *words* more efficient. They play a derivative role. This assumption profoundly mistakes how even a goods economy works, as our revisions in earlier chapters have shown. But the same assumption proves catastrophic in an economy of attention. When you waste words, you are wasting the principal scarce resource—attention. The Official Stylist wastes his own attention in adding lard, but he wastes the reader's attention as well. Attention is what, to use the popular phrase, *adds value* in an attention economy. The pompous posturing of the Official Style attacks productivity at its heart—where data is converted into productive, usable, information.

We can now introduce the most compelling reason why the Official Style continues to thrive. *Because we really don't think words matter.* They don't matter enough to make instruction in them an essential concern. And so we train ourselves not to pay attention to them. Writing badly becomes a matter of pride; hire someone else to do it if your secretary can't. A great deal of pious cant today proclaims that writing is important, *but we don't really believe it.* In an economy of attention you had better believe it. There, words matter.

This change from stuff to attention is creating strong pressures to write in the plain style. To take one example, the Securities and Exchange Commission has issued a special set of guidelines—readers of *Revising Prose* will find them familiar—for the preparation of documents being submitted to that agency. The enormous expenditure of attention required to decode the Official Style will no longer be tolerated. All across our economy, extraordinary efforts have been made to cut costs and reduce waste. It should not surprise us that the Official Style has caught the cost-cutters' gaze. Precisely the revision *Revising Prose* teaches has become a valuable talent, not simply an elegant adornment.

THE SECOND KIND

The second kind of answer is both simpler than the first and more complex. We've looked at many examples of inept writing—writing that ranges from shapeless to mindless. The second kind of answer to "Why bother?" is simply, "Are you willing to sign your name to what you have written? To present yourself in public—whether it matters to anyone else or not—as such a person?" In a sense, it is a simple question: "Whatever the advantage—or disadvantage—ought I do this?" The primary moral question: If everyone else is committing perjury, ought I do the same? Do you choose to encounter the world on its terms or on your own? A simple question but one we must all answer for ourselves.

"The style is the man," says the old adage. Perhaps it means that to this basic moral question you'll give the same answer for writing as for the rest of your behavior. Yet the question is complex, too, for what type of behavior is "prose behavior"? Prose is usually described in a moral vocabulary— "sincere," "open" or "devious," and "hypocritical"—but is this vocabulary justified? Why, for that matter, has it been so moralistic? Why do so many people feel that bad prose threatens the foundations of civilization? And why, in fact, do we think "bad" the right word to use for it?

STYLE AND SELF

Let's start with the primary ground for morality, the self. We may think of the self as both a dynamic and a static entity. It is static when we think of ourselves as having central, fixed selves independent of our surroundings, an "I" we can remove from society without damage, a central self inside our head. But it becomes dynamic when we think of ourselves as actors playing social roles, a series of roles that vary with the social situation in which we find ourselves. Such a social self amounts to the sum of all the public roles we play.

Our complex identity comes from the constant interplay of these two kinds of self. Our final "self" is usually a mixed one, few of us being completely the same in all situations or, conversely, social chameleons who change with every context. The self grows and develops through the free interplay between these two kinds of self. If we were completely sincere we would always say exactly what we think—and cause social chaos. If we were always acting an appropriate role, we would be certifiably insane. Reality, for each of us, presents itself as constant oscillation between these two extremes.

When we say that writing is sincere, we mean that somehow it has managed to express this complex oscillation, this complex self. It has caught the accent of a particular self, a particular mixture of the two selves. Sincerity can't point to any specific verbal configuration, since sincerity varies as widely as human beings themselves. The sincere writer has not said exactly what she felt in the first words that occurred to her. That might produce a revolutionary tirade, or "like, you know" conversational babble, or the gross mistakes we've been reviewing. Nor has a sincere writer simply borrowed a fixed language, as when a bureaucrat writes in the Official Style. She has managed to create a style which, like the social self, can become part of society, can work harmoniously in society and, at the same time, like the central self, can represent her unique selfhood. She holds her two selves in balance; this is what "authority" in prose means.

Now reverse this process. Writing prose involves for the writer an integration of self, a deliberate act of balancing its two component parts. It represents an act of socialization, and it is by repeated acts of socialization that we become sociable beings, that we grow up. Thus, the act of writing models the presentation of self in society; prose reality rehearses us for social reality. It is not a question of a preexistent self making its message known to a preexistent society. It is not, initially, a question of message at all. Writing clarifies, strengthens, and energizes the self, renders individuality rich, full, and social. This does not mean writing that flows, as Terry Southern immortally put it, "right out of the old guts onto the goddamn paper." Precisely the opposite. Only by taking the position of the reader toward one's own prose, putting a reader's pressure on it, can the self be made to grow into full sociability. Writing should enhance and expand the self, allow it to try out new possibilities, tentative selves.

The moral ingredient in writing, then, works first not on the morality of the message but on the nature of the sender, on the complexity of the self. "Why bother?" To invigorate and enrich your selfhood, to increase, in the most literal sense, your self-consciousness. Writing, properly pursued, does not make you better. It makes you more alive. This is why our growing illiteracy ought to distress us. It tells us something, something alarming, about the impoverishment of our selves. We say that we fear written communication will break down. Unlikely. And if it does we can always do what we do any- way—pick up the phone. Something more fundamental stands at stake, the selfhood and sociability of the communicators. We are back to the basic peculiarity of writing: it is premedi- tated utterance, and in that premeditation lives its first if not its only value. "Why bother?" "To find out who I really am." It is not only what we *think* that we discover in writing, but what we *are* and *can construct ourselves to be.*

We can now understand why the purely neutral, transpar- ent style is so hard to write and so rare, and why we take to jargon, to the Official Style, to all the varieties of poetic diction and verbal ornament, with such alacrity. We are doing more in writing, any writing, than transmitting neutral messages. We want to convey our feelings about what we say, our atti- tude toward the human relationships we are establishing. Neutral communications do not come naturally to people.

What matters most to us is our relationships with our fellow creatures. These urges continually express themselves through what we write. They energize what we call style. Style has attracted a moralistic vocabulary because it expresses all the patterns of human behavior that morality must control. This moralistic vocabulary leads to considerable confusion, but it arises naturally enough from the way human beings use literary style.

How rare a purely neutral human relationship really is you can appreciate simply by reflecting on your daily life. Is there any response, however trivial, that we don't color with hand gestures, facial expressions, postures of the body? Human beings are nonstop expressers, often through minute subconscious clues. We sense, immediately, that a friend is angry at us by the way he says "Hello." He doesn't say, "Go to hell, you skunk" instead of "Hello." He doesn't need to. Tense vocal chords, pursed lips, a curt bob of the head perhaps, do just as well. No one has put a percentage figure to this segment of human communication, but it far outranks plain statement in frequency and importance. The same truth prevails for written communication. We are always trying to say more than we actually do. This stylistic voice-over technique is our natural way of speaking. *Skotison* makes perfect sense when we consider the entire range of human expression.

VALUE JUDGMENTS

We now begin to understand what kinds of value judgments make sense about prose and what kinds don't. The prevailing wisdom teaches that the best prose style is the most transparent, the least seen; prose ideally aspires to a perfect neutrality; like the perfect secretary, it gets the job done without intruding. Such ideal prose rarely occurs. Might that be because it isn't ideal? Doesn't ideal neutrality rule out most of what we call good prose? The ideal document of perfect neutrality would be a grocery list. (And think of how we immediately flood that neutral document with likes and dislikes, with *emotions*—not sardines *again!*) We mean by "good prose" something different from impersonal transparency. We mean a style suffused with a sense of human relationships, of specific occasions and why they matter. We mean a style that expresses a genuinely complex and fully socialized self.

We've cleared up a lot of muddy writing in this book. The metaphor "clear up" is clear enough, and there is no reason not to use it, but we can now explain more precisely what we have been doing. An incoherent style is "clear enough." It depicts clearly an incoherent mind, an incoherent person. Looked at in this way, all prose is clear. Revision aims to "clear up" the *person*, to present a self more coherent, more in control. A mind thinking, not a mind asleep. It aims, that is, not to denature the human relationship that prose sets up, but to enhance and enrich it. It tries not to squeeze out the expression of personality but to make this expression possible; not to squeeze out all record of a particular occasion and its human relationships but to make them maximally clear. Again, this is why we worry so much about bad prose. It signifies incoherent people, failed social relationships. This worry makes sense only if we feel that prose, ideally, should express human relationships and feelings, not abolish them.

Think, for example, about a familiar piece of prose we might all call successful, Lincoln's *Gettysburg Address*. Its brevity has been much praised, but the brevity does not work in a vacuum. It makes sense, becomes expressive, only in relation to the occasion. Lincoln took for his subject the inevitable gap between words and deeds. At Gettysburg, this gap was enormous, and the shortness of Lincoln's speech does reverence to it. No speech could do justice to what had happened at Gettysburg. Lincoln's brevity did not remove the emotion of the occasion but intensified it; it did not ignore the occasion's human relationships but celebrated them. We think it a monument to brevity and clarity not because it neutralizes human emotion but because it so superbly enshrines the emotions that fit the occasion.

"VASCULAR DISTURBANCES" VS.
BLEEDING FROM THE EARS

We might, as a contrasting example, consider a modern instance of public prose. In 1977, the Federal Aviation Administration published a document called *Draft Environmental Impact Statement for the Proposed Public Acquisition of the Existing Hollywood-Burbank Airport*. It discussed, in two volumes and about fifteen hundred pages, the noise and pollution problems the airport caused and what might happen if the Lockheed Corporation sold it to a consortium of interested city governments. The Statement also included extensive testimony about the airport by private citizens. The Statement itself provides a perfect—if at times incomprehensible—example of the Official Style; the citizens, with some exceptions, speak and write plain English. The Statement as a whole constitutes an invaluable extended example of how the two styles conflict in real life.

The issue posed was simple. Lockheed was going to shut the airport down and sell the land if the city governments didn't buy it. Would the loss of airport jobs and public transportation be compensated by the increased peace and quiet in the East San Fernando Valley? Horrible noise on the one hand; money on the other. How do you relate them to one another? The different styles in the Statement put the problem in different ways. They seem, sometimes, to be describing different problems. So in this sample of the Statement's archetypal Official Style:

> The findings of ongoing research have shown that a number of physiological effects occur under conditions of noise exposure.... These studies demonstrate that noise exposure does influence bodily changes, such as the so-called vegetative functions, by inhibition of gastric juices, lowered skin resistance, modified pulse rate and increased metabolism....
>
> Other studies have investigated the generalized physiological effects of noise in relation to cardiovascular disturbances,

gastrointestinal problems, impairment of performance on motor tracking tasks and vascular disturbances, as well as various physical ailments. Miller (1974) states that, "Steady noise of 90 dB increases tension in all muscles." Welch (1972) concludes that "environmental sound has all-pervasive effects on the body, influencing virtually every organ system and function that has been studied," and Cohen (1971) summarized that "the distressing effects of noise alone or combined with other stress factors can eventually overwhelm man's capability for healthy adjustment with resultant physical or mental ailments...."

The VTN survey determined the presence of annoyance reactions which have been identified as indicators of stressful response to environmental noise among respondents both inside and outside the noise impact area. As is reported in Section 2.5.3 (Annoyance Reactions as Determinants of Community Response to Airport Noise) of this chapter, individuals' beliefs about the noise and the noise source tend to determine their reactions to its occurrence and the amount of disturbance it creates....

When asked for the three things they liked least about their neighborhood, 14.2 percent of the respondents in the high noise exposure area, compared to only 5.3 percent of those residing in the low noise exposure area, indicated aircraft noise among the three. It appears from these observations that Hollywood-Burbank Airport does produce annoyance reactions among residents of the East Valley, which indicates a perception of environmental stress associated with Airport noise.

No need to do a detailed analysis at this stage of the game—the formula as before. In this distanced and impersonal world, no one ever suffers; they experience "the presence of annoyance reactions." And, in the report's ever-cautious style, it only "appears" that the airport produces such reactions among residents. Later, in the residents' comments, that "appearance" becomes an oppressive reality.

Human beings, we need to remind ourselves here, are social beings. Our reality is a social reality. Our identity draws its felt life from our relation to other people. We become

uneasy if, for extended periods of time, we neither hear nor
see other people. We feel uneasy with the Official Style for
the same reason. It has no human voice, no face, no personality behind it. It creates no society, encourages no social conversation. We feel that it is unreal. The "better" it is, the more
typical, the more unreal it becomes. And so we can answer
the question of whether you can write a "good" Official Style.
Yes, of course, when you must work in the Official Style, you
can observe its conventions in a minimal way. But the closer
you get to the impersonal essence of the Official Style, the
more distant any felt human reality becomes.

But public prose need not erase human reality. It can do
the opposite, as in the following passage from the same report—a letter from a homeowners' group president. With it,
we return to human life.

> Our Homeowners Association was formed about a year and a
> half ago principally because of an overwhelming fear of what might
> happen to our homes, schools and community as a result of any
> steps which might be taken by Lockheed and/or the City of
> Burbank. Our community is inexorably linked to Hollywood-
> Burbank Airport. The northern part of the North/South runway
> is in our city....
>
> Our community consists of a vast majority of single-family
> residences, and long-time owners with "paid in full" or "almost paid
> up" mortgages. We have been told, "You moved in next to the air-
> port, it was there before you were." This is true in most cases. But,
> and this is a big "but"—it was an entirely different airport when
> most of us moved into the area. 20 to 25 years ago, the airport
> was "home" to small planes. We actually enjoyed watching them
> buzz around, and many of us spent Sunday afternoons at the air-
> port while our children were amused watching the little planes.
> However, the advent of the jet plane at HBA changed the entire
> picture. Suddenly we were the neighbors of a Noise Factory!...
>
> Our children are bombarded with noise in 2 local elementary
> schools, Roscoe and Glenwood. Teachers have to stop teaching
> until the noise passes over and everyone waits "for the next one."

If the school audiometrist wants an in-depth test for a child with questionable hearing, the child must be taken away from the school altogether to eliminate outside noises.

Our backyards, streets, parks and churches, too, are inundated with noise…noise is an ever-constant fact of life for us. There is seldom a time when one cannot hear a plane somewhere in the vicinity—it may be "up" or it may be "down," but once a motor is turned on, we hear it!

We might well be asked, "Why do you continue to live in such a place?" Put in plain and simple terms—we have no place else to go! Years have passed and we have put more money into our mortgages and into our property. We have developed long-time friendships with neighbors and the Community. We don't want to move!…

Where do we go? Who is going to pay us—and how much will we be paid—for being uprooted? Who sets the price on losing a street and an entire neighborhood full of long-time friends? If 7 schools are to be closed, where do the children go? What happens to the faculty and staff at the schools? The parochial schools? The small business man who sells consumer goods—what happens when there is no one to sell to?

A living voice! Human society! Plain English, in a context like this, takes on the moral grandeur of epic, of the high style. The language of ordinary life reasserts our common humanity. Precisely the humanity the Official Style seeks to banish. It is a bad style, then, because it denatures human relations. When we consider that it is becoming the accepted language for the organizations that govern our human relations, we perceive how stylistic and moral issues converge.

Our current literacy crisis may come, then, from more than inattention, laziness, or even the diabolical purposes of the Official Style. It may come, ultimately, from our meager ideal for prose. We say that what we want is only a serviceable tool—useful, neutral, durable, honest, practical, and so on. But none of us takes so utilitarian an attitude even toward our tools! If we earn our living with them, we love them. We clean and polish and lubricate them. We prefer one kind to another for quirky, personal reasons. We modify them. We want them not only to do a job but to express us, the attitude we take toward our job.

So, too, with prose. We hunger for ceremony, for attitude, for ornament. It is no accident that bureaucrats play games with buzzwords, build what amounts to purely ornamental patterns, create a *poetic* diction. These games express an attitude, albeit an ironically despairing one, toward what they are doing, the spirit in which they work. Jargons are created, too, for the same reason, to express a mystique, the spirit in which work is done. And, like a student's incoherence, they have their own eloquence, reflect clearly a habit of thought, a way of doing business. When we object to the prose, we are actually objecting to the habit of thought, the bureaucratic way of life. It is because, paradoxically enough, the style is so clear, so successfully communicates a style of life, that we so feel its emotional impoverishment.

"NO PROFIT IS WHERE IS
NO PLEASURE TAKEN"

We have two choices, then, in regard to prose. We can allow the expression of personality and social relationships and attempt to control them, or we can ban them and try to extinguish them. Perhaps we should try the first alternative for a while. We've tried the second for the better part of a century and we know where it leads. It leads to where we are now, to the Official Style. For those of us working alone to improve our prose, the choice is even clearer. Even if society disregards the importance of words, we must go in the other direction, train ourselves to notice them and to notice them as much as "content." A style that at first appears peculiar may not be a "bad" style but simply eloquent about an unexpected slice of reality, one that you may or may not like. Keep clear in mind when you are responding to the words and when to the situation they represent. You'll find that you do first the one and then the other. You'll be rehearsing the same oscillation we have already found to be at the base of stylistic revision. You'll have trained your pattern of attention in the same way that an artist trains his eyes or a musician her ears. After all, you can't revise what you can't see. Only by sensitizing yourself to the styles around you can you go beyond a fixed set of rules, a paramedic procedure.

In fact, in the long run, that is what any fixed set of rules ideally ought to do. It ought to guide us in training our verbal vision, expanding our intuition about words. Rules, analytic devices, are a shortcut to vision but no real substitute for being able to *see* a prose pattern. The paramedic analogy here breaks down. Beyond paramedicine lies medicine; beyond the specific analysis of specific styles—what we have been doing here—lies the study of style in general. Verbal style can no more be fully explained by a set of rules, stylistic or moral, than can the rest of human behavior. Intuition, trained intuition, figures as strongly in the one as in the other. You must learn how to see, and that learning is not entirely a rule-based proceeding.

Prose style, then, does not come down to a set of simple rules about clarity, brevity, and sincerity. It is as complicated as the rest of human behavior, and this because it forms part of that behavior as well as expressing it. People who tell you that mastering prose style is simple are kidding you. They make reading and writing grotesquely simplistic, in fact unreal. As students, all of us complained about the "unreality" of our school life, but where school life at any level is *most real*—in the vital act of verbal expression—we most yearned for simplification. Well, we can't have it both ways. You can choose the moralizing, rule-centered world, with its simplistic static conception of self and society, but you must not be surprised, when you use it in the real world, if it seems "unreal" in theory and backfires in practice.

The other road is harder. You have to read and write and pay attention to both acts. If you do, you'll begin to savor the elegance with which we humans can communicate the subtleties of behavior. You'll begin, for the first time, to become self-conscious about the language you speak and hence about the society you live in. You will become more alive. And you'll begin to suspect what is perhaps a third answer to the question, "Why bother?" Because it's fun—much more fun than writing the Official Style for the rest of your life.

APPENDIX

TERMS

You can see things you don't know the names for, but in prose style, as in everything else, it is easier to see what you know how to describe. The psychological ease that comes from calling things by their proper names has not often been thought a useful goal by modern pedagogy. As a result, inexperienced writers often find themselves reduced to talking about "smoothness," "flow," and other meaningless generalities when they are confronted by a text. And so here are some basic terms.

PARTS OF SPEECH

In traditional English grammar, there are eight parts of speech: verbs, nouns, pronouns, adjectives, adverbs, prepositions, conjunctions, interjections. *Grammar*, in its most general sense, refers to all the rules that govern how meaningful statements can be made in any language. *Syntax* refers to sentence structure, to word order. *Diction* means simply word choice. *Usage* means linguistic custom.

Verbs

1. Verbs have two voices, active and passive.
   An *active verb* indicates the subject acting:
   Jack *kicks* Bill.
   A *passive verb* indicates the subject acted upon:
   Bill *is kicked by* Jim.
2. Verbs come in three moods: indicative, subjunctive, and imperative.
   A verb in the *indicative mood* says that something is a fact. If it asks a question, it is a question about a fact:
   Jim *kicks* Bill. *Has* Bill *kicked* Jim yet?
   A verb in the *subjunctive mood* says that something is a wish, hypothetical, or contrary to fact, rather than a fact:
   If Jim *were* clever, he *would* kick Bill.
   A verb in the *imperative mood* issues a command:
   Jim, *kick* Bill.
3. A verb can be either transitive or intransitive.
   A *transitive verb* takes a direct object:
   Jim *kicks* Bill.
   An *intransitive verb* does not take a direct object. It represents action without a specific goal:
   Lori *runs* every day.
   The verb "to be" ("is," "was," and so on) is often a *linking* verb because it links subject and predicate without expressing a specific action:
   Elaine *is* a movie mogul.
4. English verbs have six tenses: present, past, present perfect, past perfect, future, and future perfect.
   Present: Jim *kicks* Bill.
   Past: Jim *kicked* Bill.
   Present perfect: Jim *has kicked* Bill.
   Past perfect: Jim *had kicked* Bill.
   Future: Jim *will kick* Bill.
   Future perfect: Jim *will have kicked* Bill.

The present perfect, past perfect, and future perfect are called compound tenses. Each tense can have a progressive form. (e.g., present progressive: Jim *is kicking* Bill.)

5. Verbs in English have three so-called infinite forms: *infinitive, participle,* and *gerund.* These verb forms often function as adjectives or nouns.
Infinitive:
   To assist Elaine isn't easy.
   (When a word separates the "to" in an infinitive from its complementary form, as in "to directly stimulate" instead of "to stimulate," the infinitive is said to be a split infinitive.)
   Participles and gerunds have the same form; when the form is used as an adjective, it is called a *participle*; when used as a noun, a *gerund*.
Participles:
Present participle:
   Elaine was in an *arguing* mood.
Past participle:
   Lori's presentation was very well *argued.*
Gerund:
   Arguing with Elaine is no fun.

Verbs that take "it" or "there" as subjects are said to be in an *impersonal construction*: "It has been decided to fire him" or "There has been a personnel readjustment."

Nouns

A noun names something or somebody. A proper noun names a particular being or place—Elaine, Pittsburgh.

1. *Number.* The singular number refers to one ("a cat"), plural to more than one ("five cats").
2. *Collective nouns.* Groups may be thought of as a single unit, as in "the army," and thus take a singular verb.

Pronouns

A pronoun is a word used instead of a noun. There are different kinds:

1. *Personal pronouns*: I, me, him,...
2. *Intensive pronouns*: myself, yourself,...
3. *Relative pronouns*: who, which, that. These must have antecedents, words they refer back to. "Lori has a talent (antecedent) that (relative pronoun) Elaine does not possess."
4. *Indefinite pronouns*: somebody, anybody, anything
5. *Interrogative pronouns*: who?, what?

Possessives

Singular: A *worker's* hat. Plural: The *workers'* hats. ("It's," however, equals "it is." **The possessive is "its"—no apostrophe!**)

Adjectives

An *adjective* modifies a noun: "Lori was a *good* hiker."

Adverbs

An *adverb* modifies a verb: "Lori hiked *swiftly* up the trail."

Prepositions

A *preposition* connects a noun or pronoun with a verb, an adjective, or another pronoun: "I ran into her arms" or "The girl with the blue scarf."

Conjunctions

Conjunctions join sentences or parts of them. There are two kinds, coordinating and subordinating.

1. *Coordinating conjunctions*—and, but, or—connect statements of equal status: "Bill ran *and* Jim fell" or "I got up *but* soon fell down."
2. *Subordinating conjunctions*—that, when, because—connect a main clause with a subordinate one: "I thought *that* they had left."

Interjections

A sudden outcry: "Wow!" or "Ouch!"

SENTENCES

Every sentence must have both a subject and verb, stated or implied: "Elaine (subject) directs (verb)."

Three Kinds

1. A *declarative sentence* states a fact: "Elaine directs films."
2. An *interrogative sentence* asks a question: "Does Elaine direct films?"
3. An *exclamatory sentence* registers an exclamation: "Does she ever!"

Three Basic Structures

1. A simple sentence makes one self-standing assertion, i.e., has one main clause: "Elaine directs films."
2. A compound sentence makes two or more self-standing assertions, i.e., has two main clauses: "Elaine directs films and Lori is a tax lawyer" or "Jim kicks Bill and Bill feels it and Bill kicks Jim back."
3. A complex sentence makes one self-standing assertion and one or more dependent assertions in the form of subordinate clauses dependent on the main clause:

"Elaine, who has just finished directing *Jim Kicks Bill*, must now consult Lori about her tax problems before she can start blocking out *Being Kicked: The Sequel*."

In *compound sentences*, the clauses are connected by *coordinating conjunctions*, in *complex sentences* by *subordinating conjunctions*.

Restrictive and Nonrestrictive Relative Clauses

A *restrictive clause* modifies directly, and so restricts the meaning of the antecedent it refers back to: "This is the tire *that blew out on the freeway*." One specific tire is referred to. Such a clause is not set off by commas, because it is needed to complete the meaning of the statement about its antecedent: "This is the tire"—what tire?

A *nonrestrictive clause*, though still a dependent clause, does not directly modify its antecedent and is set off by commas: "These tires, *which are quite expensive*, never blow out on the freeway." A nonrestrictive clause can be removed without changing the sense of the main clause: "These tires never blow out on the freeway."

Appositives

An *appositive* is an amplifying word or phrase placed next to the term it refers to and set off by commas: "Henry VIII, *a glutton for punishment*, rode out hunting even when sick and in pain."

BASIC SENTENCE PATTERNS

What words do you use to describe the basic syntactic patterns in a sentence? In addition to the basic types—declarative, interrogative, and exclamatory—and the basic forms of simple, compound, and complex, other terms sometimes come in handy.

Parataxis and Hypotaxis

Parataxis: Phrases or clauses arranged independently, in a coordinate construction, and often without connectives, e.g., "I came, I saw, I conquered."

Hypotaxis: Phrases or clauses arranged in a dependent subordinate relationship, e.g., "I came, and after I came and looked around a bit, I decided, well, why not, and so conquered."

The adjectival forms are *paratactic* and *hypotactic*, e.g., "Hemingway favors a paratactic syntax while Faulkner prefers a hypotactic one."

Asyndeton and Polysyndeton

Asyndeton: Connectives are omitted between words, phrases, or clauses, e.g., "I've been stressed, destressed, beat down, beat up, held down, held up, conditioned, reconditioned."

Polysyndeton: Connectives are always supplied between words and phrases, or clauses, as when Milton talks about Satan pursuing his way, "And swims, or sinks, or wades, or creeps, or flies."

The adjectives are *asyndetic* and *polysyndetic*.

Periodic Sentence

A periodic sentence is a long sentence with a number of elements, usually balanced or antithetical, standing in a clear syntactical relationship to each other. Usually it suspends the conclusion of the sense until the end of the sentence, and so is sometimes said to use a *suspended syntax*. A periodic sentence shows us a pattern of thought that has been fully worked out, whose power relationships of subordination have been carefully determined, and whose timing has been climactically ordered. In a periodic sentence, the mind has finished working on the thought, left it fully formed.

There is no equally satisfactory antithetical term for the opposite kind of sentence, a sentence whose elements are

loosely related to one another, follow in no particularly antithetical climactic order, and do not suspend its grammatical
completion until the close. Such a style is often called a *running style* or a *loose style*, but the terms remain pretty vague.
The loose style, we can say, often reflects a mind *in the process
of thinking* rather than, as in the periodic sentence, having
already completely ordered its thinking. A sentence so loose
as to verge on incoherence, grammatical or syntactical, is often called a *run-on sentence*.

Isocolon

The Greek word *isocolon* means, literally, syntactic units of
equal length, and it is used in English to describe the repetition of phrases of equal length and corresponding structure.
So Winston Churchill on the life of a politician: "He is asked
to stand, he wants to sit, and he is expected to lie."

Chiasmus

Chiasmus is the basic pattern of antithetical inversion, the
AB:BA pattern. President John F. Kennedy used it in his inaugural address:

A	B
Ask not *what your country*	*can do for you*, but

B	A
what you can do	*for your country.*

Anaphora

When you begin a series of phrases, clauses, or sentences
with the same word or phrase, you are using anaphora. So
Shakespeare's Henry V to some henchpersons who have be-
trayed him:

Show men dutiful?
Why, so didst thou. Seem they grave and learned?
Why, so didst thou. Come they of noble family?
Why, so didst thou. Seem they religious?
Why, so didst thou.

(*Henry V,* 2.2)

Tautology

Repetition of the same idea in different words. In many ways, the Official Style is founded on this pattern. Here's a neat example from Shakespeare:

Lepidus. What manner o'thing is your crocodile?
Antony. It is shap'd, sir, like itself, and it is as broad as it has breadth. It
   is just so high as it is, and moves with its own organs. It lives by that
   which nourisheth it, and the elements once out of it, it transmigrates.
Lepidus. What colour is it of?
Antony. Of its own colour too.
Lepidus. 'Tis a strange serpent.
Antony. 'Tis so. And the tears of it are wet.

(*Antony and Cleopatra,* 2.7)

NOUN STYLE AND VERB STYLE

Every sentence must have a noun and a verb, but one can be emphasized, sometimes almost to the exclusion of the other. The Official Style—strings of prepositional phrases + "is"— exemplifies a noun style *par excellence.* Here are three examples, the first of a noun style, the second of a verb style, and the third of a balanced noun-verb mixture.

Noun Style

There is in turn a two-fold structure of this "binding-in." In the first place, by virtue of internalization of the standard, conformity with it tends to be of personal, expressive and/or instrumental significance to ego. In the second place, the structuring of the reactions of alter to ego's action as sanctions is a function of his conformity with the standard. Therefore conformity as a direct mode of the fulfillment of his own need-dispositions tends to coincide with the conformity as a condition of eliciting the favorable and avoiding the unfavorable reactions of others.

(Talcott Parsons, *The Social System* [Glencoe, Ill.: Free Press, 1951], p. 38)

Verb Style

Patrols, sweeps, missions, search and destroy. It continued every day as if part of sunlight itself. I went to the colonel's briefings every day. He explained how effectively we were keeping the enemy off balance, not allowing them to move in, set up mortar sites, and gather for attack. He didn't seem to hate them. They were to him like pests or insects that had to be kept away. It seemed that one important purpose of patrols was just for them to take place, to happen, to exist; there had to be patrols. It gave the men something to do. Find the enemy, make contact, kill, be killed, and return. Trap, block, hold. In the first five days, I lost six corpsmen—two killed, four wounded.

(John A. Parrish, *12, 20 & 5: A Doctor's Year in Vietnam* [Baltimore: Penguin Books, 1973], p. 235)

Mixed Noun-Verb Style

We know both too much and too little about Louis XIV ever to succeed in capturing the whole man. In externals, in the mere business of eating, drinking, and dressing, in the outward routine of what he loved to call the *métier du roi*, no historical character, not even Johnson or Pepys, is better known to us; we can even, with the aid of his own writings, penetrate a little of the majestic façade which is Le Grand Roi. But when we have done so, we see as in a glass darkly. Hence the extraordinary number and variety of judgments which have been passed upon him; to one school, he is incomparably the ablest ruler in modern European history; to another, a mediocre blunderer, pompous, led by the nose by a succession of generals and civil servants; whilst to a third, he is no great king, but still the finest actor of royalty the world has ever seen.

(W. H. Lewis, *The Splendid Century: Life in the France of Louis XIV* [New York: Anchor Books, 1953], p. 1)

PATTERNS OF RHYTHM AND SOUND

Meter

The terms used for scanning (marking the meter of) poetry sometimes prove useful for prose as well.

> *iamb*: unstressed syllable followed by a stressed one, e.g., in vólve.
> *trochee*: opposite of iamb, e.g., úse fŭl.
> *anapest*: two unstressed syllables and one stressed syllable, e.g., per son nél.
> *dactyl*: opposite of anapest, one stressed syllable followed by two unstressed ones, e.g., óp er ate.

These patterns form *feet*. If a line contains two feet, it is a *dimeter*; three, a *trimeter*; four, a *tetrameter*; five, a *pentameter*; six, a *hexameter*. The adjectival forms are *iambic, trochaic, anapestic,* and *dactylic*.

Sound Resemblances

Alliteration: This originally meant the repetition of initial consonant sounds but came to mean repetition of consonant sounds wherever they occurred, and now is often used to indicate vowel sound repetition as well. You can use it as a general term for this kind of sound play: "Peter Piper picked a peck of pickled peppers"; "Bill will always swill his fill."

Homoioteleuton: This jawbreaker refers, in Latin, to words with similar endings, usually case-endings. You can use it to describe, for example, the "shun" words—"function," "organization," "facilitation"—and the sound clashes they cause.

For further explanation of the basic terms of grammar, see George O. Curme's *English Grammar* in the Barnes & Noble College Outline Series. For a fuller discussion of rhetorical terms like *chiasmus* and *asyndeton*, see Richard A. Lanham's *A Handlist of Rhetorical Terms* (second edition, Berkeley and Los Angeles: University of California Press, 1991). For a fuller discussion of prose style, see Richard A. Lanham's *Analyzing Prose* (New York: Scribner's, 1983).

INDEX

Patton, General George, 64
Periodic style, 70–75, 123–124
Phibbs, Brendan, 63, 68
Plain-language laws, viii
Plato, 91
PM. *See* Paramedic Method
Polysyndeton, 123
Possessives, 120
Prepositional-phrase strings, 3,
    24, 78
  examples of, discussed, 5–12,
    15–17, 35–36, 48–49,
    51–52, 62, 93–95,
    96–97
Prepositions, 120
Pronouns, 120

Q
Quintilian, 81, 102

R
Reading aloud, 34, 53, 58–60,
    66–67, 68–69, 90
Relative clauses, 122

S
Securities and Exchange
    Commission, viii, 103
Self-consciousness, stylistic, x,
    58, 66, 92, 100,
    113–115
Sentence length, 63–64, 88
Sentence rhythm, 11, 55–57,
    62, 64–67, 74–75, 98
Sentence shape, 10–11, 24–50
    passim, 52–53, 72–73,
    93–94

Sentences, basic kinds of,
    121–124
Shakespeare, William
  Antony and Cleopatra, 125
  Henry V, 125
Sincerity, 105–106
Skotison, 81–82, 84
Southern, Terry, 106
Syntax, defined, 117

T
Tautology, 125
Tin ears, 55–57
Tricolon crescens, 56, 60
Truscott, General Lucien, 64
Typography, 67, 80, 88, 89–90,
    93–99

U
Usage, defined, 117

V
Verbs, 118–119
Verb style, 126

W
Wooldridge, Adrian, 79
Word processors. *See*
    Computers

Y
Yablonsky, Lewis, 70